A
TASTE
OF
THE
HOLIDAYS

compiled
by
Dot Gibson

A River Oaks Book

Copyright © 1988
By
Dot Gibson Publications
Waycross, Georgia

ISBN 0-941162-07-9

Additional copies may be obtained from

A Taste of the Holidays
P.O. Box 935
Waycross, Georgia 31502

8th printing 1998, over 95,000 copies in print

Printed in the U.S.A.
By

FATHER&SON
ASSOCIATES, INC.
4909 N. Monroe Street
Tallahassee, Florida 32303

CONTENTS

Every recipe a Holiday Treat — for relatives,
friends, or your own special family.

BREADS

Banana Nut Bread

1	cup sugar	1	teaspoon soda
1	stick margarine	2	large or 3 small bananas
2	eggs	1	teaspoon vanilla
1½	cups flour	1	cup chopped nuts

Cream sugar and margarine. Add eggs one at a time. Combine flour and soda; add to mixture. Add mashed bananas, vanilla and nuts. Pour into greased and floured loaf pan. Bake at 350 degrees for 40 to 50 minutes.

Carrot Bread

1	cup vegetable oil or margarine	2	cups sugar
4	eggs	4	teaspoons baking powder
2	teaspoons vanilla	½	teaspoon soda
2	cups grated carrots	½	teaspoon salt
3	cups flour	2	cups chopped pecans

Beat eggs, add oil, vanilla and carrots. Combine flour, sugar, baking powder, soda, salt and nuts. Add to egg mixture and blend well. Pour into 2 greased and floured loaf pans. Bake at 350 degrees for 1 hour to 1 hour 10 minutes, or until done. Cool in pan for 10 minutes.

Pumpkin Bread

1	cup oil	1	teaspoon baking powder
2⅔	cups sugar	2	teaspoons baking soda
4	eggs	1	teaspoon salt
1	16-ounce can pumpkin	1	teaspoon cinnamon
⅔	cup water	1	teaspoon nutmeg
3	cups flour	1	cup chopped nuts

Beat oil and sugar; add eggs one at a time. Mix in pumpkin and water. Mix together flour, baking powder, soda, salt, cinnamon, and nutmeg; add to mixture. Mix only until moist. Stir in nuts. Pour into greased loaf pans and bake 350 degrees 1 hour or until cake tester comes out clean when inserted in center.

Cherry Pecan Bread

1	stick margarine	1	cup buttermilk
¾	cup sugar	1	teaspoon vanilla
2	eggs	1	cup chopped pecans
2	cups flour	1	10-ounce jar maraschino
1	teaspoon baking soda		cherries
½	teaspoon salt		

Drain and chop cherries. Set aside. Cream sugar and margarine. Add eggs one at a time and beat well. Sift together flour, soda, and salt. Add to creamed mixture alternately with buttermilk. Stir in vanilla, nuts and cherries. Pour into a greased 9 × 5-inch loaf pan. Bake at 350 degrees for 55 to 60 minutes.

OPTION: glaze with powdered sugar icing if desired.

Peanut Butter Bread

1½	cups flour	½	cup chunky peanut butter
1	cup sugar	1	egg
3	teaspoons baking powder	1	cup oatmeal
½	teaspoon salt	1	cup milk

Combine flour, sugar, baking powder and salt. Cut in peanut butter as you would shortening. Beat egg and add; mix in milk and oats. Stir until just moistened. Pour into greased 9 × 5 loaf pan. Bake at 350 degrees for 1 hour.

Zucchini Bread

3	eggs	3	cups sifted flour
1	cup vegetable oil	1	teaspoon soda
2	cups sugar	¼	teaspoon baking powder
2	sups grated, unpeeled zucchini	1	teaspoon salt
		2	teaspoons cinnamon
1	teaspoon vanilla	1	cup chopped pecans

Beat eggs until light and foamy. Gradually add oil and sugar, mixing well. Add zucchini and vanilla. Mix lightly, but well. Sift together flour, soda, baking powder, salt and cinnamon. Add to creamed mixture. Mix just until moistened. Stir in pecans. Pour into 2 greased and floured 9 × 5-inch loaf pans. Bake at 325 degrees for 1 hour or until well done.

Strawberry Nut Bread

Pretty and delicious

4	eggs	3	cups flour
2	cups sugar	1	teaspoon cinnamon
1	cup cooking oil	1	teaspoon baking soda
2	10-ounce packages frozen strawberries	1	teaspoon salt
		1	cup chopped nuts

Beat eggs until fluffy; add sugar, oil and thawed strawberries. Combine flour, cinnamon, soda, and salt; sift together. Add to egg mixture and mix well. Stir in nuts. Pour into 2 greased and floured loaf pans. Bake at 350 degrees for 1 hour 10 minutes.

For that little extra, serve with strawberry butter. Mix 2 sticks margarine with ½ cup strawberry jam; blend.

Blueberry Muffins

1	cup blueberries	¾	teaspoon salt
2	tablespoons sugar	¾	cup milk
1¾	cups flour	⅓	cup vegetable oil
½	cup sugar	1	egg
2½	teaspoons baking powder		

Mix blueberries with 2 tablespoons sugar and set aside. In a large bowl stir together flour, ½ cup sugar, baking powder and salt. In separate bowl beat egg until foamy; add milk and oil. Stir egg mixture into flour. Do not over mix. Stir just enough to moisten. Fold berries into batter. Batter will be lumpy. Spoon into greased or paperlined muffin tins. Fill about ⅔ full and bake in a 400 degree oven for 20 to 25 minutes.

YIELD: 12 muffins

6 Weeks Bran Muffins

15-ounce box Raisin Bran cereal	1 teaspoon salt
3 cups sugar	4 eggs, beaten
5 cups flour	1 cup vegetable oil
5 teaspoons soda	1 quart buttermilk

Mix cereal, sugar, flour, soda and salt in a large bowl. Add egg, oil and milk. Store in a covered container in refrigerator and use when needed. Batter will keep up to 6 weeks. Fill greased muffin tins 2/3 full. Bake at 400 degrees for 15 to 20 minutes.

Lemon Yogurt Muffins

3/4 cup sugar	1 egg
1½ cups flour	3/4 stick margarine, melted
1 teaspoon soda	4 tablespoons lemon juice
1 teaspoon baking powder	1/2 cup chopped nuts (optional)
1/4 teaspoon salt	
8 ounces yogurt	

Combine sugar, flour, baking soda and powder together. In separate bowl beat together yogurt, egg, melted margarine and lemon juice. Stir into dry mixture until just blended. Stir in nuts. Spoon into greased or paper lined muffin cups. Bake at 350 degrees for 25 minutes or until pick inserted in center comes out clean.

Pecan Muffins

1½ cups flour	1 egg, slightly beaten
1/2 cup sugar	1/2 cup milk
1/2 cup chopped pecans	1/4 cup vegetable oil
2 teaspoons baking powder	1 teaspoon vanilla
1/2 teaspoon salt	

Combine flour, sugar, chopped nuts, baking powder and salt in a large bowl. Beat egg slightly, blend in milk, oil and vanilla. Pour into a well in the center of the flour mixture. Stir mixture just until moistened. Fill greased muffin cups 2/3 full. Bake at 400 degrees for 20 to 25 minutes.

Sour Cream Muffins

2	cups self rising flour	2	sticks butter, melted
1	cup sour cream		

Stir sour cream into flour. Add melted butter. Bake in regular or tiny greased muffin tins at 400 degrees for 15 minutes. These muffins freeze well. Reheat at 300 to 325 degrees.

Cinnamon Buns

1	package yeast		FILLING:
½	cup water, warm	3	tablespoons butter
½	cup milk, scalded	¼	cup sugar
⅓	cup sugar	2	teaspoons cinnamon
1	teaspoon salt	½	cup raisins, optional
2	tablespoons margarine, melted	1	cup powdered sugar
		½	teaspoon vanilla
1	egg	1	tablespoon milk
3½	cups flour		

Add yeast to warm water to soften. Combine hot milk, sugar, salt and melted margarine; cool to lukewarm. Add half of flour and beat. Add yeast and egg; beat well. Add remaining flour. Turn out on floured surface and knead very lightly until smooth. Place in a well greased bowl, cover and let rise in a warm place until doubled in bulk. Punch down and roll out in a rectangle about 9 × 18. Brush with melted butter. Combine cinnamon and sugar; sprinkle over dough. Add raisins if desired. Roll up jelly roll fashion. Pinch dough to help roll stay together. Cut into 1½-inch slices. Place in greased cake pan with a little space between rolls. Let rise until doubled.

Bake at 350 degrees 20 to 25 minutes. Cool slightly. Combine powdered sugar, vanilla and milk to form glaze — pour over top.

Christmas Stollen

1	package dry yeast	1	tablespoon grated lemon rind
¼	cup warm water		
1	cup milk	5	cups sifted flour
½	cup butter or margarine	3	tablespoons melted butter
1	egg	2	teaspoons cinnamon
¼	cup sugar	¼	cup sugar
1	teaspoon salt		
1	cup raisins		GLAZE:
½	cup chopped candied fruit	1	cup powdered sugar
½	cup chopped nuts	1 to 2	tablespoons milk
1	tablespoon grated orange rind	1	tablespoon margarine
		½	teaspoon vanilla

Soften yeast in warm water. Heat milk to scalding; remove from heat, add butter and stir until melted. Mix in egg, sugar and salt. Cool to lukewarm. Add raisins, fruit, nuts and rinds; stir. Gradually add flour to form a stiff dough. Turn out on lightly floured surface and knead until smooth. Place in a greased bowl, cover and let rise in warm place until doubles in bulk. Punch down, divide into 3 parts. Roll each to a rectangle about 16 × 9 inches; brush with melted butter. Combine sugar and cinnamon; sprinkle over melted butter on dough. Roll up and place on greased cookie sheet in shape of wreath. Pinch ends together. Cut deep gashes, 1 inch apart, all around the outside of the wreath — almost through the ring but not quite to the center holes. Turn slices slightly to open cut more. Cover and let rise until double in size about 1 hour. Bake at 350 degrees for 30 minutes.

GLAZE: Combine sugar, milk, margarine and vanilla. Pour over wreath when cooked.

Vienna Cinnamon Loaf

½	cup warm water
1	package dry yeast
¼	cup sugar
1	teaspoon salt
2	sticks margarine
6	eggs
4½	cups sifted flour

FILLING:

3	tablespoons margarine
⅔	cup brown sugar, packed
2	egg yolks
2	tablespoons milk
¼	teaspoon vanilla
2	cups finely chopped nuts
½	cup melted margarine
	Powdered sugar

Heat water to 105 to 110. Put in large bowl. Sprinkle yeast over water; stir until dissolved. Add sugar, salt, softened margarine, eggs and 3 cups of flour. Beat until smooth, about 4 minutes. Add remaining flour and again beat until smooth. Cover and let rise in a warm place until doubles, about 2 hours. Place in refrigerator overnight. For filling stir together margarine, brown sugar, and yolks. Stir in milk and vanilla. Fold in nuts. Stir down dough. Turn out on floured surface. Work with half of dough keeping other half in refrigerator. Roll first half into a 14 × 9-inch rectangle. Brush with melted margarine. Spread half of filling over dough. Roll from both sides to center making a 9-inch loaf. Turn over with smooth side up and place in greased pan. Brush top with melted margarine. Repeat for second loaf. Cover, let rise 1½ hours or until doubles in size. Bake at 350 degrees for 35 minutes. Remove from pan. Sprinkle with powdered sugar.

Gingerbread Waffles

1	cup molasses	1	egg	
⅓	cup margarine	2	cups flour	
1½	teaspoons soda	2	teaspoons ginger	
½	cup sour milk	1	teaspoon salt	

Combine molasses and margarine and bring to a boil. Remove from heat and cool to lukewarm. Add soda, milk and well beaten egg. Sift together flour, ginger and salt; add to mixture. Do not have waffle iron too hot. Serve with whipped cream.

YIELD: 8 waffles

Candle Stick Bread

1½ cups all-purpose flour
2 teaspoons baking powder
1 teaspoon salt
½ teaspoon soda
½ teaspoon cinnamon
½ cup sugar
1 cup uncooked oats
1 cup diced candied fruit

⅓ cup chopped pecans
2 eggs, beaten
3 tablespoons vegetable oil
1 cup milk
Powdered sugar
Milk
Candied cherries

Combine flour, baking powder, salt, soda and cinnamon. Stir in sugar, oats, candied fruit and nuts. In separate bowl mix eggs, oil and milk. Add to dry ingredients and stir just until dry ingredients are moistened. Pour into 6, well-greased 6-ounce metal cans (such as individual fruit juice or frozen fruit juice). Fill about ⅔ full. Place on cookie sheet and bake at 350 degrees for 35 to 40 minutes. Cool in cans for 10 minutes before removing. Mix a little powdered sugar with milk; drizzle over top of candle bread. Stand a cut piece of cherry in top for flame.

Flower Pot Bread

½ cup milk
3 tablespoons margarine or butter
1½ cups water

5½ cups flour
3 tablespoons sugar
2 teaspoons salt
1 package dry yeast

Combine milk, butter and water; heat until warm. In large bowl combine 2 cups of flour, sugar, salt and dry yeast; mix well. Gradually add warmed liquid to flour mixture. Beat well. Add 1 cup flour and continue to beat. Add the rest of flour to form a soft dough. If more is needed add an additional ½ to 1 cup. Turn out on floured surface; knead until smooth. Place in greased bowl, cover and let it rise until doubles in bulk approximately 1 hour. Punch down and turn out on floured surface. Separate into four pieces. Roll out to small rectangles 4 × 6. Fold under and push into greased 3-inch floured pots. Let double in size and bake at 400 degrees for 25 to 30 minutes. Remove from pot to cool — replace into pot for serving.

YIELD: 4 – 3-inch pots of bread

Monkey Bread

4 tubes Buttermilk Biscuits	1½ tablespoon cinnamon, divided
2 cups sugar, divided	1 stick margarine

Cut each biscuit into four pieces. Combine 1 cup sugar, 1 tablespoon of cinnamon in plate or plastic bag. Roll or shake each biscuit piece in sugar mixture. Layer in a greased tube pan. Sprinkle remaining sugar over top. Combine margarine, 1 cup sugar and ½ tablespoon of cinnamon in small sauce pan; heat until boiling. Pour over biscuits in pan. Bake at 350 degrees for 40 to 45 minutes. Let cool 5 to 10 minutes. Loosen sides and invert on serving plate. Serve hot.

Angel Biscuits

5 cups flour	1 cup shortening
3 teaspoons baking powder	¼ cup warm water
1 teaspoon salt	1 package dry yeast
1 teaspoon soda	2 cups buttermilk
¼ cup sugar	

Add yeast to warm water to dissolve 10 to 12 minutes. Combine flour, baking powder, salt, soda, and sugar in large bowl. Cut in shortening. Combine yeast with buttermilk and add to flour mixture. Mix until smooth. Turn out on lightly floured surface and roll to ¾-inch thickness. Cut to desired size. Bake at 400 degrees for 12 to 15 minutes.

Sausage Biscuit

¾ pound hot ground pork
  sausage
2⅔ cups flour
2 tablespoons sugar
1 teaspoon baking powder
½ teaspoon soda
½ teaspoon salt
½ cup shortening
1 package dry yeast
¼ cup warm water
1 cup buttermilk
Melted butter or margarine

Cook sausage in a heavy pan until browned and broken into small pieces. Place on paper towel to drain. Mix flour, sugar, baking powder, soda and salt in a large bowl. Cut in shortening until like coarse meal. Dissolve yeast in water; let stand about 5 minutes. Combine yeast and buttermilk, stirring well. Add to the flour mixture and stir until moistened. Add sausage and knead into dough. Place dough on a lightly floured board and knead lightly several times to get sausage mixed throughout. Roll to about ½-inch thickness. Cut and place on ungreased pan. Brush top with melted margarine. Bake in a 425 degree oven about 10 minutes or until light brown. Biscuits can be frozen before baking. Remove from freezer when needed, baked while still frozen 425 degrees for 10 minutes.

Sausage Roll

A great gift for Christmas morning

4 cups flour
¼ cup corn meal
¼ cup sugar
2 tablespoons baking powder
¼ teaspoon salt
⅔ cup vegetable oil
½ cup milk
2 pounds ground sausage
  meat

Combine flour, meal, sugar, baking powder and salt. Sift together in large bowl. Stir in vegetable oil. Add milk and blend. Add a couple extra tablespoons of milk if necessary to form a stiff dough. Roll in a rectangle on a lightly floured surface. Spread on sausage and roll jelly-roll fashion lengthwise. Wrap in waxed paper and chill or freeze. When ready to use slice and bake at 350 degrees for 15 to 20 minutes.

 # CAKES

Elegant Cheesecake

Fantastic plain or with glaze

CRUST:
3/4 cup coarsely ground nuts
3/4 cup graham cracker crumbs
3 tablespoons melted butter or margarine

FILLING:
4 (8-ounce) packages cream cheese
1 1/4 cups sugar
4 eggs
1 tablespoon lemon juice
2 teaspoons vanilla

TOPPING
2 cups sour cream
1/4 cup sugar
1 teaspoon vanilla

GLAZE:
1 pint strawberries
1 12-ounce jar strawberry or raspberry jelly
1 tablespoon cornstarch
1/4 cup water
1/4 cup cointreau (optional)

CAKE: Combine nuts, crumbs and butter; press firmly in bottom of 9 or 10-inch spring form pan. Beat cream cheese in mixer until light and fluffy. Beat in sugar until smooth. Add eggs, one at a time. Add lemon juice and vanilla and beat well. Spoon filling over crust. Set pan on cookie sheet and bake at 350 degrees, 10-inch pan 40 to 50 minutes, 9-inch 50 to 55 minutes. Remove from oven, let stand 15 minutes. Combine sour cream, sugar and vanilla; blend well. Spoon over top, spread to within 1/2 inch of edge. Return to 350 degree oven for 5 minutes. Let cake cool completely then refrigerate at least 24 hours (better if 2 days).

GLAZE: A couple hours before serving wash and hull berries; dry. Combine jelly with cornstarch in sauce pan and mix well. Add remaining jelly, water and Cointreau. Cook over medium heat, stir until thickens and clears, (about 5 minutes). Cool. Using knife loosen cake from pan; remove spring form. Arrange berries on top of cake spoon glaze over berries and drip down sides. Return to refrigerator.

Christmas Coconut Cake

CAKE:
1 cup butter, softened
2 cups sugar
4 eggs
3 cups all-purpose flour
2 teaspoons baking powder
Dash of salt
1 cup milk
1 teaspoon vanilla
1 teaspoon coconut flavoring

COCONUT FROSTING:
1 cup milk
¼ cup all-purpose flour
½ cup butter, softened
½ cup shortening
1 cup sugar
1 teaspoon coconut flavoring
1 teaspoon vanilla flavoring
2 cups flaked coconut, divided
Red and green candied cherries optional for decoration

CAKE: Cream butter; add sugar, and beat 10 to 15 minutes. Add eggs, one at a time, beating well after each addition. Combine flour, baking powder and salt; add to creamed mixture alternately with milk beginning and ending with flour mixture. Mix well after each addition. Stir in flavorings. Pour batter into 3 greased and floured 9-inch round cake pans. Bake at 350 degrees for 20 to 25 minutes or until a pick inserted in center comes out clean. Cool cake in pans 10 minutes. Remove from pans and let cool completely.

COCONUT FROSTING: Combine milk and flour in a medium saucepan; cook over medium heat, stirring constantly, until mixture thickens. Remove saucepan from heat, and let mixture cool completely. Add butter, shortening and sugar; beat well. Add vanilla and coconut flavoring and 1 cup coconut, stirring well. Spread frosting between layers and on top and sides of cake. Sprinkle top and sides with remaining 1 cup coconut. Garnish with cherries if desired. Cover and chill before serving.

Fresh Apple Cake

Hot, cold, plain or frosted

CAKE:
1½ cups Wesson oil
2 cups sugar
3 eggs
3 cups cake flour
½ teaspoon salt
1 teaspoon soda
2 teaspoons vanilla
1 cup chopped pecans
3 cups finely chopped apples

FROSTING:
1 stick margarine
1½ cups brown sugar
1 cup white sugar
½ cup powdered sugar
½ cup evaporated milk
10 to 12 marshmallows

CAKE: Combine oil, sugar and eggs; mix well. Sift together flour, salt and baking soda. Add to mixture. Add vanilla and fold in nuts and apples. Grease and flour pan. Can be baked in a bundt or tube pan at 350 degrees for 1 hour to 1¼ hours, a 13 × 9 × 2-inch pan at 350 degrees for about 45 minutes or 3, 8-inch cake pans for 35 minutes or 2 loaf pans for about 45 minutes.

FROSTING: Mix all ingredients, except marshmallows, in pan and boil for about 4 minutes. Add marshmallows and stir until melted. Beat until thick enough to spread.

Sour Cream Coconut Cake

The Famous Rotten Cake

1 box yellow cake mix
2 layer size

FROSTING:
1 pint sour cream, divided
1 cup sugar

1 teaspoon vanilla
1 9-ounce carton frozen non-dairy topping
2 6-ounce package frozen coconut

Bake cake as directed on box. Cool and slice layers in half to make 4 thin layers. Combine 1 cup sour cream, sugar, vanilla and 1 package of coconut. Spread between layers. Combine 1 cup sour cream and thawed topping mix. Spread on top and sides of cake. Sprinkle with remaining coconut. Place in airtight container and refrigerate for 3 days (leave to "Rot".) Outstanding!!

Banana Nut Layer Cake

CAKE:

1   stick plus 1 tablespoon
    margarine
1½ cups sugar
3   eggs
4   ripe bananas, mashed
1   tablespoon baking soda
⅓   cup plus 1 tablespoon
    buttermilk
2   teaspoons vanilla
2   cups flour
2   teaspoons baking powder
½   teaspoon salt
¾   cup nuts

FROSTING:

1   stick margarine
8   ounces cream cheese
1   box 10x powdered sugar
1   teaspoon vanilla
1   cup chopped nuts

CAKE: Cream margarine and sugar until smooth and creamy. Add eggs, one at a time, beating after each addition. In separate bowl blend mashed bananas and baking soda; add buttermilk and vanilla. Add this banana mixture to creamed mixture. Sift together flour, salt, and baking powder. Stir flour into batter until smooth and well blended. Add nuts. Pour into 2 greased 9-inch cake pans and bake at 350 degrees for 20 to 25 minutes.

FROSTING: Cream margarine and cream cheese until light and fluffy. Beat in sugar and add vanilla. Frost tops and sides of layers. Sprinkle nuts on top of cake.

Good cake but need to use bought frosting.

Roseanna Banana Cake

CAKE:
- ⅔ cup margarine
- 1⅔ cups sugar
- 3 eggs
- 1¼ cups mashed bananas
- 2¼ cups flour
- 1¼ teaspoons baking powder
- 1¼ teaspoons soda
- 1 teaspoon salt
- ⅔ cup buttermilk
- ⅔ cup chopped nuts

BROWN SUGAR FROSTING:
- 1 cup packed brown sugar
- ½ cup margarine, melted
- ¼ cup milk
- 3 cups sifted powdered sugar

CAKE: Cream margarine and sugar until light and fluffy; blend in eggs and bananas. Combine flour, baking powder, soda, and salt. Add buttermilk and flour mixture alternately to butter mixture, mixing well after each addition. Stir in nuts. Pour into greased and floured 13 × 9-inch baking pan. Bake at 350 degrees 45 to 50 minutes or until cake tester inserted in center comes out clean. Cool and frost with Brown Sugar Frosting.

FROSTING: Combine brown sugar, margarine and milk in saucepan; bring to a boil, stirring constantly. Remove from heat; cool 10 minutes. Gradually add powdered sugar, beating until well blended.

Elmer Fudpucker Cake

CAKE:
- 1 18-ounce box Orange Supreme cake mix
- ½ cup oil
- 1 3½-ounce box vanilla instant pudding
- ¼ cup vodka
- ¼ cup apricot nectar
- ¼ cup apricot brandy
- 4 eggs

FUDPUCKER TOPPING:
- 1 cup powdered sugar
- 2 tablespoons apricot nectar
- 2 tablespoons vodka
- 2 tablespoons apricot brandy

Combine all cake ingredients, using cake and pudding mixes dry, and beat 4 minutes. Pour into a well greased and lightly floured bundt pan. Bake at 350 degrees for 45 to 50 minutes. Mix topping ingredients and heat. Pour over hot or cooled cake.

Hummingbird Cake

CAKE:

3   cups flour
2   cups sugar
1   teaspoon soda
1   teaspoon salt
1   teaspoon cinnamon
3   eggs, beaten
1   cup vegetable oil
1½ teaspoons vanilla
1   cup chopped nuts
1   8-ounce can crushed
    pineapple, with juice
2   cups chopped bananas

FROSTING:

1   8-ounce package cream
    cheese
1   stick margarine or butter
1   16-ounce box powdered
    sugar
1   teaspoon vanilla
½   cup chopped nuts

CAKE: Mix flour, sugar, soda, salt and cinnamon and set aside. Beat eggs and add vegetable oil. Stir egg mixture into dry ingredients. Stir until well mixed. Add vanilla, nuts, pineapple, with juice, and bananas. Pour into 3 greased and floured 9-inch pans. Bake at 350 degrees for 25 to 30 minutes. Cool.

FROSTING: Set cream cheese and butter our to soften; combine and beat until smooth. Add powdered sugar and vanilla. Beat until light and fluffy. Frost cake and sprinkle chopped nuts on top.

"Blue Ribbon" Lemon Cheese Cake

CAKE:
1   cup butter
2   cups sugar
3   eggs
3   cups cake flour
½   teaspoon soda
1   teaspoon vanilla
1   cup buttermilk

LEMON-CHEESE FILLING:
1   cup sugar
1   cup water
2   egg yolks
2   tablespoons flour
½   stick butter
3   lemons, grated and juiced

FLUFFY WHITE ICING:
2   egg whites
½   cup water
1½ cups sugar
1   tablespoon corn syrup
1   teaspoon cream of tartar
1   teaspoon vanilla
Dash of Salt

CAKE: Cream butter and sugar. Add eggs one at a time, beating after each egg. Combine and sift flour and soda. Add flour and buttermilk alternately to mixture. Pour into 4 greased and floured cake pans. Bake at 350 degrees for 25 to 30 minutes. Remove from pans and cool.

FILLING: Blend all ingredients in the top of a double broiler and cook over medium heat until thickened. Cool and spread over cake layers.

ICING: Place all ingredients in top of double boiler and cook over boiling water, beating with electric mixer for 7 minutes or until mixture forms stiff peaks. Spread around sides of cake.

SERVES: 20

Caramel Layer Cake

A favorite

CAKE:
¾ cup butter, softened
2 cups sugar
4 eggs
3 cups sifted cake flour
2 teaspoons baking powder
1 cup milk
1 teaspoon vanilla

CARAMEL FROSTING:
3 cups sugar
2 cups whipping cream
¼ cup butter
¼ cup light corn syrup
1 tablespoon vanilla

CAKE: Cream butter and sugar, beating until light and fluffy. Add eggs one at a time. Combine flour and baking powder. Add dry ingredients to creamed mixture alternately with milk, beginning and ending with flour mixture. Add vanilla and mix well. Pour into 2 greased and floured 9-inch cake pans. Bake at 350 degrees for 25 to 30 minutes. Cool in pans 10 minutes; remove from pans and cool completely.

FROSTING: Combine all ingredients except vanilla in a buttered heavy saucepan; cook over medium heat until a candy thermometer reaches 240 degrees (soft ball) stir often. Let cool slightly; add vanilla, and beat until spreading consistency. Spread between layers and on top and sides of cake.

Italian Cream Cake

CAKE:
1   stick margarine
½   cup vegetable shortening
2   cups sugar
5   eggs, separated
2   cups plain flour
1   teaspoon soda
1   cup buttermilk
1   teaspoon vanilla
1   small can coconut
1   cup chopped nuts

FROSTING:
1   8-ounce package cream cheese
1   stick margarine
1   box powdered sugar
1   teaspoon vanilla
Chopped nuts

CAKE: Cream margarine and shortening. Add sugar and beat until light and smooth. Add egg yolks and beat well. Combine flour and soda and add to butter mixture alternately with buttermilk, starting and ending with flour. Add vanilla and stir in coconut and nuts. Fold in egg whites last. Pour into 3 greased and floured 8 or 9-inch cake pans and bake at 350 degrees for 25 minutes.

FROSTING: Beat cream cheese and margarine until smooth. Add sugar and mix well. Add vanilla and beat until all is well blended. Add a little milk if needed. Spread on cake and sprinkle with nuts.

Kahlua Angel Food

Great Way to Liven up a Bought Cake

1   Angel Food cake
2   tablespoons Kahlua
¼   cup Kahlua

¼   cup cream
1   16-ounce tub Cool Whip

Purchase Angel Food Cake. Poke holes all over top of cake with thin knife or skewer. Combine 2 tablespoons Kahlua and ¼ cup cream and pour half of it into holes. Place cake in refrigerator for 2 hours. Pour the rest of Kahlua and cream mixture into holes and refrigerate 2 more hours. Combine Cool Whip, ¼ cup Kahlua and spread on top and side of cake — serve.

Toasted Butter Pecan Cake

CAKE:
3 tablespoons butter or margarine
1⅓ cups chopped pecans, divided
¾ cup butter or margarine
1 ⅓ cups sugar
1½ teaspoons vanilla
2 eggs
2 cups sifted flour
2 teaspoons baking powder
¼ teaspoon salt
⅔ cup milk

BUTTER PECAN FROSTING:
4 tablespoons butter or margarine
3 cups sifted powdered sugar
2½ to 3 tablespoons light cream
1 teaspoon vanilla
Nuts

CAKE: Spread 3 tablespoons of butter over pecans and toast at 350 degrees for 15 minutes; stir occasionally. Cream ¾ cup butter and gradually add sugar. Beat until light and fluffy. Add vanilla and beat in eggs, one at a time. Sift together flour, baking powder, and salt; add dry ingredients to creamed mixture, alternately with milk. Fold in 1 cup of toasted nuts; save ⅓ cup for top of cake, Pour batter into 2 greased and floured 8-inch cake pans. Bake at 350 degrees for 30 to 35 minutes. Cool partially, remove from pans and cool completely.

FROSTING: Combine butter, sugar, cream and vanilla; beat until smooth and creamy. Frost cake and sprinkle nuts on top.

Nutty Cake

⅓ cup vegetable oil
⅔ cup sugar, divided
1½ cups sifted cake flour
1½ teaspoons baking powder
½ teaspoon salt
½ cup milk
1 egg
1 teaspoon vanilla
½ cup finely chopped pecans

Cream oil with ⅓ cup sugar. Combine in separate bowl sifted flour, baking powder and salt. Add dry ingredients, ¼ cup at a time, alternately with milk, into oil mixture; begin and end with dry ingredients. Beat about 30 seconds or until smooth after each addition. Combine egg, remaining ⅓ cup sugar and vanilla and beat until thick. Fold into batter. Spread chopped nuts over bottom of a lightly greased 8-inch square pan. Carefully pour in batter and bake at 350 degrees for 30 to 35 minutes. Cool 10 minutes. Cut into squares.

Carrot Cake

CAKE:

4	eggs
1	cup vegetable oil
2	cups flour
2	cups sugar
2	teaspoons soda
1	teaspoon salt
2	teaspoons cinnamon
4	cup grated raw carrots (about 8 carrots)
½	cups chopped pecans

CREAM CHEESE FROSTING

1	stick margarine
	8-ounce package cream cheese
4⅓	cups sifted powder sugar
1	teaspoon vanilla
1	teaspoon maple (optional)

CAKE: In a large bowl beat eggs until light. Slowly beat in oil. In a separate bowl combine flour, sugar, soda, salt and cinnamon; stir until mixed well. Gradually add dry ingredients; beat until smooth. Pour into 3 greased and floured 8-inch cake pans. Bake at 350 degrees for 25 to 35 minutes or until done. Cool in pans for 10 minutes; remove from pan and cool completely before frosting.

FROSTING: Blend softened margarine and cream cheese. Gradually add powdered sugar, beating until creamy. Stir in vanilla and maple.

YIELD: 1 3-layer cake

Yule Log

5 eggs, separated	Sweetened whipped cream or
½ cup sugar	frozen whipped topping
3 tablespoons cocoa	Powdered sugar
3 tablespoons flour	Option—Mocha Butter
1 teaspoon vanilla	Cream—for frosted Log see below

Grease a 15 × 10 × 1-inch pan; cover bottom with wax paper and grease paper heavily. Separate eggs and beat whites until stiff. Beat egg yolks in large bowl at high speed. Gradually add sugar and beat until light and foamy. Add cocoa, flour, and vanilla beating at low speed. Fold in egg whites. Pour batter onto wax paper and spread evenly in pan. Bake at 350 degrees for 15 to 20 minutes. Bake until cake springs back when lightly pressed with fingers. Remove from oven, turn out onto towel that has been sprinkled with powdered sugar. Remove wax paper. Roll cake lengthwise with towel while cake is warm. Let stand 5 minutes. Unroll and fill with thawed topping or whipped cream. Reroll, place seam down and dust with powdered sugar.

Elegant Yule Log

A little fancier

1 baked Yule Log cake	1 tablespoon unsweetened
2 sticks butter	cocoa
½ cup powdered sugar	1 tablespoon instant coffee
	1 teaspoon water

Beat butter until fluffy. Beat in sugar and cocoa. Dissolve coffee in water and beat into butter mixture. When you unroll the cake spread with 3 or 4 tablespoons of Mocha Cream and top this with frozen topping. Reroll lengthwise using towel to help roll. Place on serving plate seam side down. Frost log with remaining Mocha Butter Cream. Make bark designs in frosting with fork or spatula. Sprinkle lightly with powdered sugar. Refrigerate.

Mississippi Mud Cake

Sinfully Delicious

CAKE:
2 cup sugar
2 sticks butter or margarine
4 eggs
1½ cups flour
⅓ cup cocoa
⅛ teaspoon salt
1½ cups chopped pecans
1 teaspoon vanilla
Miniature marshmallows to cover cake

FROSTING:
1 stick margarine (melted)
⅓ cup evaporated milk
⅓ cup cocoa
1 pound box powdered sugar
1 teaspoon vanilla
1 cup chopped nuts

CAKE: Cream sugar and butter. Add eggs one at a time and beat well. Sift flour, cocoa, and salt together and add to creamed mixture mixing well. Add vanilla and nuts. Pour into a greased and floured 13 × 9-inch pan and bake at 300 or 350 degrees for 35 minutes. Remove from oven and spread marshmallows on top. Return to oven until marshmallows have melted about 10 minutes. Cool and frost.

FROSTING: Combine margarine, milk and cocoa in saucepan. Cook on low heat until melted. Add sugar and mix until smooth. Add vanilla and nuts. Spread on cake.

Easy Chocolate Sheet Cake

CAKE:

2   cups flour
2   cups sugar
2   sticks margarine
1   cup water
4   tablespoons cocoa
½   cup buttermilk
2   eggs
1½   teaspoons soda
1   teaspoon vanilla

FROSTING:

1   stick margarine
⅓   cup milk
4   tablespoons cocoa
1   pound box powdered sugar
½   cup chopped pecans
1   teaspoon vanilla

CAKE: Combine flour and sugar in a large bowl. Combine margarine, water, and cocoa in a sauce pan and bring to a boil. Pour cocoa mixture into flour and beat until well mixed. Add milk, eggs, soda and vanilla. Pour into greased 9 × 13-inch pan and bake at 350 degrees for 30 minutes.

FROSTING: Combine margarine, milk and cocoa in sauce pan and bring to a boil. Remove from heat. Add powdered sugar and stir until well mixed. Add nuts and vanilla. Spread on cake while still in pan.

Black Forest

CAKE:
3   eggs
5   egg yolks
Pinch salt
1   teaspoon vanilla
¾   cup sugar
1   cup sifted cake flour
¼   cup cocoa powder
½   stick butter, melted

FROSTING:
1   quart whipping cream
Sugar
1 to 2 tablespoons cornstarch
Kirsch, (an unaged cherry
      brandy)
1   can bing cherries

CAKE: Combine eggs, 5 yolks, salt, vanilla, and sugar in top of double boiler. Whip until mixture reaches 110 degrees. Remove from over hot water but continue beating until mixture reaches maximum volume and starts to thin slightly. Fold in flour and cocoa. Fold in melted butter. Pour into 3 greased and floured 8-inch pans. Bake at 350 degrees for 30 minutes.

FROSTING: Whip cream with enough sugar to sweeten. Place cherries in pan on stove. Add sugar to sweeten lightly and thicken with cornstarch. Set off to cool. Place first layer on plate. Sprinkle liberally with Kirsch. Pipe a row of cream around outer edge to serve as dam for cherries. Pour cherries and slightly thickened cherry juice on layer. Place 2nd layer on. Sprinkle with Kirsch and spread ½-inch layer of whipped cream on. Place 3rd layer on. Sprinkle with Kirsch and spread a thin layer of cream on top and all around sides.

Chocolate Pastry Cake

2   4-ounce packages sweet
     baking chocolate
½   cup sugar
½   cup water

2   teaspoons vanilla
     10-ounce package pie crust mix
2   cups heavy cream

Shave 3 squares of chocolate for decorations. Set aside. (Use carrot peeler dipped in hot water). Combine remaining chocolate, sugar and water in small sauce pan over low heat. Stir until melted and smooth. Remove from heat; add vanilla and allow to cool to room temperature. Stir ¾ cup of chocolate mix into dry pie crust. Stir until smooth. Divide in fourths and press each out into 8-inch circle. Easiest way is to press out over outside bottom of 8-inch round cake pan to about ¼ inch from edge. Bake at 425 degrees for 6 to 8 minutes or until almost firm. Trim if spread over edges so all will be the same size. Cool about 5 minutes and remove from pan with spatula. Cool completely. Whip cream, fold in remaining chocolate and spread between layers and on top of cake. Place chocolate shavings on top and place in refrigerator covered to chill for at least 8 hours.

SERVES: 12 to 14

Black Russian Cake

CAKE:
1   deep chocolate cake mix,
     2-layer size
1   3¾-ounce box instant
     chocolate pudding
¾   cup strong coffee
¾   cup Cream de Cocoa and
     Kaluha combined
4   eggs

TOPPING:
1   cup powdered sugar
2   tablespoons coffee
2   tablespoons Creme de
     Cocoa
2   tablespoons Kaluha

CAKE: Combine all cake ingredients and beat until well mixed, about 4 minutes. Pour into a greased bundt pan and bake 45 to 50 minutes. Use temperature recommended on cake mix.

TOPPING: Mix all ingredients and heat. Pour hot glaze topping over hot cake. Punch holes in cake top with long skewer or cake tester so that glaze can run into cake.

Lane Cake

A beautiful cake for the holidays

CAKE:
1   cup butter or margarine
2   cups sugar
1   teaspoon vanilla
3¼ cups flour
3½ teaspoons baking powder
1   cup milk
8   egg whites

WHITE FLUFFY FROSTING:
1   cup sugar
⅓   cup water
Dash of cream of tartar
Dash of salt
2   egg whites
1   teaspoon vanilla

FILLING:
8   egg yolks
1   cup sugar
½   cup butter or margarine
1   cup chopped nuts
1   cup raisins
½   cup marachino cherries, cut
1   cup coconut
¼ to ⅓ cup wine, bourbon, or liqueur

CAKE: Cream butter and sugar until light and smooth, add vanilla. Sift flour and baking powder together. Add to creamed mixture alternately with milk, beating well after each addition. Fold in egg whites. Pour into 3 greased and floured 9-inch pans and bake at 350 degrees for 20 to 25 minutes or until done. Cool in pans 10 minutes; remove from pans and cool completely.

FILLING: Combine yolks, sugar and butter in saucepan over low heat. Stir over low heat until mixture thickens. Remove from heat and add remaining ingredients. Cool to room temperature. Spread on tops of layers only.

FROSTING: In sauce pan combine sugar, water, cream of tartar and salt. Bring to boil. Beat egg whites and slowly add syrup. Add vanilla. Beat about 7 minutes until peaks form. Spread around side of cake.

Easy Amaretto Cake

CAKE:
1½ cups chopped toasted almonds, divided
1 18-ounce yellow cake mix (without pudding)
1 (3½-ounce) package vanilla instant pudding mix
½ cup water
½ cup vegetable oil
4 eggs
½ cup amaretto
1 teaspoon almond extract

GLAZE:
½ cup sugar
¼ cup water
2 tablespoons butter or margarine
¼ cup amaretto
½ teaspoon almond extract

CAKE: Sprinkle 1 cup of almonds in bottom of well-greased and floured 10-inch tube pan. In large mixer bowl combine cake mix, and pudding mix. Beat in water, oil and eggs. Add amaretto, almond flavoring and remaining ½ cups almonds. Beat about 4 minutes. Pour batter into tube pan. Bake in preheated oven at 350 degrees for 1 hour or until cake tester is inserted and comes out clean. Cool cake in pan about 15 minutes and remove.

GLAZE: Combine sugar, water and margarine in small sauce pan and bring to a boil. Reduce heat and cook for 4 to 5 minutes for sugar to dissolve. Remove from heat and cool 15 to 20 minutes and add amaretto and almond. Stick holes in top of cake with skewer or cake tester. Spoon glaze over cake allowing it to run into holes.

Pistachio Cake

Easy, pretty and so moist

CAKE:
1 box white cake mix 2-layer size
¾ cup vegetable oil
¾ cup water
4 eggs
1 3-ounce box Pistachio instant pudding
½ cup chopped nuts

GLAZE:
½ cup hot water
1 tablespoon butter, melted
2 cups powdered sugar
½ teaspoon vanilla

CAKE: Combine cake mix, oil, water, eggs and pudding mix. Beat about 4 minutes at medium speed. Pour into greased and floured 9 × 13 × 2-inch pan. Sprinkle top with nuts. Bake at 350 degrees for 35 to 40 minutes.

GLAZE: Place water, butter, powdered sugar and vanilla in small bowl and beat with a fork. While cake is still hot punch holes with a fork over the entire top. Spoon icing over cake allowing it to run down into holes. Pry holes open if necessary to insure that the icing runs into cake. Is a pretty green, stays moist and is a real favorite.

Poppy Seed Loaf Cake

CAKE:
½ cup butter or margarine
1 cup sugar
¼ cup poppy seeds
1 teaspoon vanilla extract
2 eggs
1½ cups all-purpose flour
1 teaspoon baking powder
½ teaspoon salt
½ cup half-and-half

GLAZE:
1 cup sifted powdered sugar
½ teaspoon vanilla extract
Juice of 1 lemon or lime

CAKE: Cream butter until light. Add sugar gradually, beating until light and fluffy. Add poppy seeds, vanilla, and eggs. Beat until well mixed. Combine flour, baking powder, and salt. Add dry ingredients alternately with cream to the butter mixture, beginning and ending with dry ingredients. Pour into a greased and floured 8½ × 4½-inch loaf pan. Bake at 350 degrees for 50 minutes or until pick inserted in center comes out clean. Cool in pan 10 minutes, remove and pour glaze over warm cake.

GLAZE: Combine sugar, vanilla and lemon juice and mix well. Pour over cake.

Queen Elizabeth Cake

CAKE:
1   cup chopped dates
1   cup boiling water
1   teaspoon baking soda
¼   cup butter
1   cup sugar
2   eggs
1½ cups flour
1   teaspoon vanilla
½   cup chopped nuts

ICING:
5   tablespoons sugar
5   tablespoons evaporated
    milk
2   tablespoons butter
Toasted coconut and nuts

CAKE: Pour boiling water over chopped dates. Let stand until cool and then add baking soda. Cream butter and sugar well. Add eggs, flour, vanilla and nuts. Add date mixture. Pour into a long flat pan or a loaf pan and bake at 350 degrees for 25 to 30 minutes.

ICING: Combine sugar, milk, and butter in pan and boil until thick, approximately 3 minutes, spread on top of cake and sprinkle with coconut and nuts.

Seven-Up Cake

CAKE:
1   18-ounce lemon cake mix
1   3½-ounce box instant
    lemon pudding mix
¾   cup oil
4   eggs
1   10-ounce 7-up

ICING:
1½ cups sugar
3   tablespoons flour
2   eggs
1   stick margarine
1   20-ounce can crushed
    pineapple
1   3½-ounce can coconut
½   cup chopped nuts

Beat eggs and oil together, blend in mixes and add 7-up last. Pour into 3 greased and floured pans and bake at 350 degrees for 20 minutes.

ICING: Combine sugar, flour, slightly beaten eggs, margarine and drained pineapple in sauce pan. Cook over low heat until thickens. Add coconut and nuts. Frost tops and sides of layers.

Rum Cake

CAKE:

1	18½-ounce package yellow cake mix
1	3¾-ounce package instant vanilla pudding mix
4	eggs
½	cup cold water
½	cup oil
½	cup dark rum
1	cup chopped pecans

GLAZE:

1	stick butter
¼	cup water
1	cup granulated sugar
½	cup dark rum
	Whipped cream—optional

Cake: Combine cake mix and pudding mix in large mixing bowl. Add eggs, water, oil and rum. Grease and flour a 10-inch tube pan. Sprinkle nuts in bottom of pan and pour batter over nuts. Bake 1 hour in a 325 degree preheated oven.

GLAZE: Melt butter in sauce pan. Mix in water and sugar. Boil 5 minutes stirring constantly. Remove from heat and stir in rum.

Invert cooled cake on plate. Stick holes in cake and drizzle glaze over top and sides. Allow cake to absorb glaze, then continue until all glaze is used. Garnish with whipped cream.

Shoofly Cake

4	cups flour		2	cups warm water
2	cups sugar		1	teaspoon baking soda
2	sticks butter or margarine		1	cup molasses

Combine and mix flour, sugar and butter. Reserve 1 cup of this mixture for topping. Mix water, soda, and molasses; add to remaining flour and sugar mixture. Pour batter into a greased 9 × 13-inch pan. Sprinkle reserved topping evenly over batter. Bake at 350 degrees for 45 minutes.

Waldorf Cake

Beautiful, moist and rich

CAKE:
½ cup butter or margarine
1½ cups sugar
2   eggs
1   teaspoon vanilla
2   tablespoons cocoa
2   (1-ounce) bottles red food
    coloring
2¼ cups sifted flour
½   teaspoon salt
1   cup buttermilk
1   teaspoon soda
1   tablespoon vinegar

WALDORF ICING:
½   cup flour
1½ cups milk
1½ cups butter
1½ cups powdered sugar
1½ teaspoons vanilla

CAKE: Cream butter and sugar. Add eggs one at a time; add vanilla. Make a paste of cocoa and food coloring; beat into mixture. Combine flour and salt; add to mixture alternately with buttermilk. Blend soda and vinegar and add to batter. Pour into greased and floured 9-inch pans. (Make 4 very thin layers or 2 layers and split to make 4 after cake has cooled.)

ICING: Cook flour and milk over low heat until pasty; cool. Cream sugar and butter, add vanilla and paste. Whip in mixer until like whipped cream. Spread between layers, top, and sides.

Almond Whipping Cream Cake

CAKE:
1 cup whipping cream
2 eggs
1 cup sugar
1 teaspoon vanilla
1½ cups sifted cake flour
2 teaspoons baking powder
¼ teaspoon salt

FROSTING:
3 ounces cream cheese, softened
1 cup sifted powered sugar
½ teaspoon almond extract
1 cup slivered almonds toasted

CAKE: Beat whipping cream until peaks form. Add eggs and beat until smooth. Add sugar and continue beating until well mixed. Add vanilla. Combine flour, baking powder, and salt. Fold dry ingredients into cream mixture. Pour into a greased and floured 8-inch square pan and bake at 375 degrees for 25 minutes or until pick inserted in center comes out clean. Cool.

FROSTING: Beat cream cheese until light. Add powered sugar and continue beating until smooth. Add almond flavoring. Stir in almonds and spread on cake.

Sponge Cake

With Broiled Caramel Icing

CAKE:
2 eggs, beaten
1 cup sugar
1 cup sifted flour
1 teaspoon baking powder
½ cup scalded milk
2 tablespoons butter
1 teaspoon vanilla

CARAMEL ICING:
3 tablespoons butter
3 tablespoons cream
½ cup dark brown sugar
1 cup chopped pecans

CAKE: Beat eggs, add sugar and continue beating until lemon colored. Add flour and baking powder that have been sifted together. Melt butter in milk and add. Add vanilla and pour into a greased and floured 8 × 8-inch pan. Bake at 350 degrees 30 to 35 minutes. Remove from oven.
ICING: Melt butter, add cream and sugar and boil for 2 minutes or until thick. Remove from heat, pour on hot cake and add nuts. Return to oven and broil 1 to 3 minutes.

A Breeze of a Pound Cake

3   sticks of butter or   6   eggs
    margarine   1   teaspoon vanilla
1   1-pound box powdered   1   teaspoon lemon extract
    sugar
Sugar box of sifted flour
    (approximately 3 cups)

Cream margarine, add powdered sugar and beat until creamy, light and fluffy. Add eggs one at a time, mixing well after each. Add sifted flour in several additions, mix just until blended each time. Add vanilla and lemon. Pour into greased and floured tube pan or 2 loaf pans. Bake in preheated oven at 325 degrees for 1¼ to 1½ hours. Loaf pans for 1 hour to 1¼ hours or until pick inserted in center comes out clean. Cool in pan about 10 minutes—turn out on rack.

Cream Cheese Pound Cake

3   sticks margarine   1   teaspoon lemon (optional)
8   ounces cream cheese   6   eggs
3   cups sugar   3   cups sifted flour
Dash of salt   1½ cups chopped pecans
1   teaspoon vanilla   (optional)

Cream margarine, cream cheese and sugar until light and fluffy. Add salt, vanilla and lemon flavoring. Beat well. Add eggs one at a time, beating well after each addition. Stir in flour. If nuts are desired add at this time. Pour into greased and floured tube pan or two loaf pans. Bake at 300 degrees for 1 hour, 20 minutes (about 1 hour for loaf pans) or until pick inserted in center comes out clean.

Chocolate Pound Cake

3 sticks butter or margarine
3 cups sugar
6 eggs
3 cups flour
⅛ teaspoon salt

½ cup cocoa
½ teaspoon baking powder
1 cup milk
1½ teaspoon vanilla

Cream butter and sugar until light and fluffy. Add eggs one at a time, beat well after each. Sift flour, salt, cocoa and baking powder together. Alternately add dry ingredients and milk to butter mixture. Add vanilla.

Pour into a greased and floured tube pan and bake for 1 hour and 15 minutes to 1 hour 30 minutes at 325 degrees. Remove from pan immediately.

Coconut Pound Cake

3 sticks butter or margarine
3 cups sugar
6 eggs
1½ teaspoons vanilla or 1 coconut flavoring

1½ teaspoons almond
3 cups flour
½ teaspoon baking powder
1 cup milk
1 7-ounce can flaked coconut (2 cups)

Cream margarine and sugar until light and fluffy. Add eggs one at a time. Beat well after each addition. Add flavorings. Sift together baking powder and flour. Add flour alternately with milk. Beginning and ending with flour. Fold in coconut. Pour into a greased and floured 10-inch tube pan and bake at 325 degrees for 1 hour and 15 minutes to 1 hour and 25 minutes.

Sour Cream Pound Cake

2 sticks butter or margarine
3 cups sugar
6 eggs, separated
3 cups flour

¼ teaspoon soda
½ pint sour cream
1 teaspoon vanilla

Cream butter and sugar well. Add egg yolks one at a time. Sift together flour and soda. Add flour and sour cream (alternately) to mixture. Add vanilla. Beat egg whites stiff and fold into batter. Pour into a greased and floured tube pan and bake at 300 degrees for 1½ hours. Remove from pan at once.

Sour Cream Coffee Cake

CAKE:
1   stick margarine
1   cup sugar
2   eggs
2   cups flour
1½ teaspoons baking powder
1   teaspoon soda
½   teaspoon salt
1   cup sour cream
1   teaspoon vanilla

TOPPING:
¾   cup brown sugar
¾   cup chopped nuts
1½ teaspoons cinnamon

GLAZE: (OPTIONAL):
½   cup powdered sugar
1   to 2 teaspoons milk

Soften margarine, add sugar and blend well. Add eggs one at a time, beating well after each addition. Combine flour, baking powder, soda and salt. Add to creamed mixture alternately with sour cream. Add vanilla. In separate bowl combine all ingredients for topping. Grease and flour a 10-inch tube pan or a flat 12 × 8-inch cake pan. For flat pan pour half of batter in pan, sprinkle on half of topping mix, and swirl with knife. Add remaining batter and top it with remaining half of topping mix. Bake at 350 degrees; 35 to 40 minutes. If using tube or bundt pan divide batter in thirds. Place ⅓ batter, ½ topping, ⅓ batter, topping and ⅓ batter. Bake at 350 degrees 45 to 60 minutes. Invert cake and add glaze. If using tube or bundt pan glaze looks attractive on inverted cake. Test with pick.

White Fruit Cake

1   cup butter
2   cups sugar
6   eggs
½   cup bourbon
4   cups flour, divided

2   teaspoons baking powder
1   pound candied cherries
1   pound candied pineapple
2   cups chopped nuts

Cream butter and sugar. Add eggs one at a time beating well after each addition. Add bourbon. Combine 3½ cups flour and baking powder, add to mixture. Roll fruit and nuts in remaining ½ cup flour. Add to batter. Bake in a 10-inch tube pan at 275 degrees for 3 to 3½ hours.

CANDY

The Best Fudge Ever

A little more trouble but oh! so good

2 cups sugar	Pinch of salt
¾ cup evaporated milk	2 tablespoon light corn syrup
2 1-ounce squares unsweetened chocolate, grated	1 tablespoon butter or margarine
	1 teaspoon vanilla

Heat milk, add grated chocolate and stir until melted. Combine sugar and salt in a heavy kettle or saucepan. Pour milk over sugar; add syrup and cook over low heat. Stir vigorously until sugar is dissolved. Increase heat and stir only until mixture boils. Boil gently. Occasionally dip to bottom and use a folding motion. Cook until reaches 234 degrees on candy thermometer or until it forms a soft ball when dropped into a cup of cold water. Remove from heat, add butter and set aside until it cools to room temperature. Beat vigorously with a spoon. Add vanilla and continue beating until it loses its shine and gloss and begins to thicken. Add nuts and pour onto buttered waxed paper or buttered 12 × 8-inch pan. When completely cooled, cut.

Opera Fudge

2 cups sugar	1 tablespoon corn syrup
⅛ teaspoon salt	1 teaspoon vanilla
¾ cup cream	¾ cup chopped nuts
½ cup milk	1 6-ounce bag semisweet chocolate morsels

Combine sugar, salt, cream, milk and syrup in heavy saucepan. Cook over medium low heat stirring until mixture boils. Boil until syrup reaches 236 degrees on candy thermometer. Pour into clean saucepan without scraping bottom of pan. Set aside to cool to lukewarm; do not stir. Add vanilla and nuts; beat with spoon until candy begins to thicken and loses its gloss. Pour into buttered 8 × 8-inch pan. Cool. Melt chocolate in double boiler. Stir until melted. Pour over white fudge. Cool until firm. Cut into squares.

Easiest of Fudge

3   6-ounce packages of semi-
    sweet chocolate morsels
1   14-ounce can condensed milk

1½ teaspoons vanilla
½   cup chopped pecans

Combine chocolate and milk. Heat until chocolate melts. Stir constantly. Remove from heat. Stir in vanilla and nuts. Pour into a greased 8 × 8-inch pan. Chill until firm. Store in refrigerator.

Cherry Nut Fudge

1   5.3-ounce can of evaporated
    milk
1⅔ cups sugar
½   teaspoon salt
1   cup miniature
    marshmallows

1   6-ounce bag semi-sweet
    chocolate chips
1   teaspoon vanilla
½   cup chopped nuts
½   cup glazed cherries
    (optional)

Mix milk, sugar and salt in sauce pan. Cook over low heat to boiling. Boil 5 minutes stirring constantly. Remove from heat. Add marshmallows, chocolate morsels, and stir well until melted. Add vanilla and nuts. Pour into a buttered 9 × 5-inch pan and cool. Cut into squares.

Turtles

1   package candy caramels
    squares
1   tablespoon butter
1   tablespoon water

1   cup chopped pecans
1   6-ounce package semi-
    sweet chocolate chips
½   block paraffin

Melt caramels with butter and water in the top of a double boiler. Add nuts. Drop by teaspoons onto a buttered cookie sheet to cool. Melt chocolate chips and paraffin in the top of a double boiler. When thoroughly blended dip cooled caramels in chocolate to cover completely. Place on wax paper to cool. Store in cooled place.

Holiday Divinity

3	cups sugar	1	3½-ounce package cherry-
¾	cup light corn syrup		or lime-flavored gelatin
¾	cup water	1	teaspoon vanilla
¼	teaspoon salt	1	cup chopped nuts
2	egg whites	½	cup flaked coconut

Butter sides of a heavy saucepan. Combine sugar, corn syrup, water and salt in pan; mix well. Cook, stirring constantly until sugar dissolves and mixture comes to a boil. Cook without stirring to hard ball stage (250 degree). Remove from heat. Beat egg whites until soft peaks form. Gradually beat in dry gelatin until stiff peaks form. Pour hot syrup slowly over egg whites, while beating at high speed until soft peaks form; add vanilla. Stir in nuts and coconut. Drop from tablespoon onto waxed paper. Makes about 60 candies.

Divinity

2½	cups sugar	2	egg whites
½	cup water	1	teaspoon vanilla
½	cup light corn syrup	1	cup finely chopped nuts
⅛	teaspoon salt		

Combine sugar, water and syrup in a large heavy saucepan. Bring to a boil, stirring only until sugar is dissolved. Continue boiling, without stirring until syrup reaches 240 degrees. A few minutes before syrup is ready combine egg whites and salt. Beat until stiff. Slowly pour in a thin stream ½ of syrup into whites, while beating. Return remaining syrup to heat and boil until it reaches 260 degrees. Add this half slowly to mixture while beating. Continue to beat until it loses gloss. Add vanilla and fold in nuts. Drop by tablespoon on to waxed paper. Swirl to form peak. Decorate with halved candied cherries.

Caramel Divinity Dream

2½ cups granulated sugar
½ cup light corn syrup
½ cup water
¼ teaspoon salt
2 egg whites
1 teaspoon vanilla

CARAMEL:
¾ cup brown sugar
1⅓ cups granulated sugar
1¼ cups evaporated milk, divided
⅛ teaspoon baking soda

Combine sugar, corn syrup, water and salt in a medium sauce pan. Cook, stirring constantly until sugar dissolves. Continue cooking until it reaches hard ball stage, 260 degrees on candy thermometer. Meanwhile beat egg whites until stiff peaks form. Gradually pour syrup over egg whites while beating at high speed. Add vanilla and beat until candy thickens and holds shape. Butter hands and shape into ¾-inch balls. Let stand until firm.

CARAMEL: In large heavy saucepan stir together sugars, 1 cup milk and soda. Cook and stir over medium heat until sugar is dissolved and mixture boils. Boil, stirring frequently until it reaches 230 degrees the soft ball stage. Remove from heat and cool without stirring to 100 degrees. Beat until thickens and loses gloss. Beat in remaining ¼ cup evaporated milk. If caramel becomes too stiff stir in a little extra evaporated milk. To coat, dip ball, one at a time into caramel. Place on waxed paper to cool.

YIELD: 6 dozen

Old-Fashioned Peanut Brittle

2 cups sugar
1 cup light corn syrup
½ cup water
4 tablespoons butter or margarine
2 cups raw peanuts, chopped
1 teaspoon baking soda

In a large heavy sauce pan heat together sugar, syrup, and water. Stir until sugar dissolves. Boil on medium to medium high until syrup reaches approximately 250 degrees; add nuts. Continue to boil and stir until it reaches 305 degrees. Syrup will be yellow brown and peanuts will pop and brown slightly. Remove from heat, add soda and butter; stir well. Pour onto 2 large greased aluminum foil strips. As candy begins to cool pull outer edges to strech. When cooled, break into pieces.

Lousianna Pralines

1½ cups granulated sugar
1½ cups light brown sugar, firmly packed
¼ cup corn syrup
⅛ teaspoon salt
1 cup evaporated milk
4 tablespoon margarine
1 teaspoon vanilla
1½ cups broken pecans

Combine the sugars, corn syrup, salt, milk and margarine in a large, heavy saucepan. Cook over medium heat stirring constantly until sugar is dissolved. Stir frequently until mixture reaches 236 degrees on candy thermometer or until it forms a soft ball when dropped in cold water. Remove from heat and cool for 2 or 3 minutes. Add vanilla and nuts and beat with wooden spoon until mixture begins to thicken. Quickly drop by spoonfuls onto greased foil. Allow to cool.

Chocolate Covered Cherries

48 maraschino cherries, with stems
3 tablespoons margarine
3 tablespoons light corn syrup
⅛ teaspoon salt
2 cups sifted powder sugar
1 tablespoon margarine
1 12-ounce bag semisweet chocolate morsels

Drain cherries and roll on paper towels to dry; set aside. Stir together softened margarine, syrup and salt; mix well. Add sugar and mix with hands until smooth. Mold about ½ teaspoon of sugar mixture around each cherry, leaving stems exposed. Place in refrigerator for 2 hours to chill. Melt chocolate and margarine in top of double boiler. Using stem to handle cherries, dip each in chocolate. Place on waxed paper. Chill until firm then place in airtight container in refrigerator.

Chocolate Covered Pretzels

1 6-ounce package milk chocolate morsels
2 tablespoons margarine
24 3-inch pretzels

Melt chocolate and margarine in top of double boiler, stir while melting. Remove from heat. Dip each pretzel in chocolate, allow excess to drain. Place on waxed paper. Chill until firm. Store in air-tight container with waxed paper between each layer.

Chocolate Creams

CREAMS:

2 1-pound boxes powdered
   sugar
1 14-ounce can condensed
   milk
1 tablespoon butter, melted
1 teaspoon vanilla
¼ teaspoon salt
2 cups finely chopped nuts

CHOCOLATE COATING:

4 squares chocolate
¼ cake paraffin

Combine all ingredients for creams and mix well. Roll into small balls and let stand in refrigerator over night. Melt chocolate and paraffin in top of double boiler. Spear each ball with pick and dip into chocolate allowing excess to drip over pan. Place on waxed paper.

Buck Eyes

1 cup butter
2 cups powdered sugar
2 cups creamy peanut butter

1 12-ounce package chocolate
   morsels

Melt butter and peanut butter in sauce pan. Add sugar and stir until melted and smooth. Refrigerate 1 hour. Form into small balls and return to refrigerator for 2 hours. Melt chocolate morsels. Spear each ball with toothpick and dip into melted chocolate. Place on waxed paper until to set. Store in refrigerator.

Tempting Truffles

4 cups powdered sugar
8 ounces cream cheese, softened
5 1-ounce squares unsweetened chocolate, melted

1 teaspoon vanilla
1 cup toasted almonds, finely chopped
1 cup powdered sugar, sifted

Soften cream cheese and gradually add sugar. Mix well after each addition. Add chocolate and vanilla. Mix well. Place in refrigerator to chill for 2 hours. Roll into 1-inch balls. Roll each ball in almonds and powdered sugar.

Chocolate Bourbon Balls

6 ounces semisweet chocolate morsels
½ cup bourbon
3 tablespoon light corn syrup

2½ cups vanilla wafer crumbs
½ cup sifted powdered sugar
1 cup finely chopped nuts

Melt chocolate in top of double boiler. Remove from heat, stir in bourbon and syrup. In separate bowl combine and mix well the crumbs, powdered sugar and chopped nuts. Add to chocolate mixture and mix well. Let stand for 30 to 40 minutes. Form into 1-inch balls and roll in sugar. Keep in refrigerator in air-tight container.

Butterscotch Crunchies

One the kids can make

12 ounces butterscotch morsels

3 ounces chow mein noodles
1 cup salted peanuts

Melt butterscotch morsels on low heat. Add chow mein noodles and peanuts. Mix well. Drop by spoonfuls on waxed paper. Chill 15 minutes.

Supreme Rocky Road

12	ounces chocolate chips	1	bag miniature
2	sticks butter		marshmallows
4	cups sugar	2	cups nuts
1½	cups evaporated milk	1	teaspoon vanilla

Spread ½ bag of marshmallows on tray, freeze. In large bowl, cut butter into small pieces; stir in chocolate chips. Set aside. Bring to boil the sugar, milk and remaining ½ bag of marshmallows. Boil rapidly 5 minutes, stirring constantly. Pour over chocolate chips and butter; stir until thick. Add nuts, vanilla and frozen marshmallows. Pour into buttered 8 × 12-inch pan.

Christmas Gems

2	16-ounce packages powdered sugar, sifted	CHOCOLATE ICING:	
1	3⅓-ounce can flaked coconut	1	1-ounce square unsweetened chocolate
1	cup chopped nuts	2	tablespoons milk
1	4-ounce bottle maraschino cherries, drained and chopped	1	tablespoon butter or margarine
1	egg white	¾	cup sifted powdered sugar
3 to 4	tablespoons milk		
1	tablespoon vanilla		

Combine powdered sugar, coconut, nuts, cherries, egg white, milk and vanilla. Mix thoroughly with hands until mixture holds together; add more milk if necessary. Press into 9 × 9-inch pan.

Combine chocolate, milk and margarine. Heat and stir until chocolate is melted; beat in powdered sugar. Spread over first layer. Chill. Cut into small bars.

Marshmallow Popcorn Balls

¾ stick margarine
3   cups miniature
     marshmallows

3   tablespoons cherry flavored
     gelatin
3   quarts popped corn,
     unsalted

Melt margarine over medium-low heat. Add marshmallows; stir until melted. Blend in dry gelatin. Pour over popcorn, mixing well. Butter hands and form into balls.

YIELD: 12 3-inch balls

Pop Corn Balls

4   quarts popped corn
1   cup sugar
1   cup light corn syrup
¼   cup water

¼   teaspoon salt
3   tablespoons margarine
1   teaspoon vanilla

Combine sugar, syrup, water, salt and margarine in small sauce pan. Cook over medium heat, stirring until sugar dissolves and mixture boils. Continue cooking, without stirring, until it reaches 250 degrees on candy thermometer (hard-ball stage.) Remove from heat and add vanilla. Pour slowly over popped corn in large bowl and mix to coat all kernels. Work quickly and shape into 4-inch balls. (As you are working with part of corn you can keep remaining in oven at 200 degrees to stay warm and pliable.) Place square of waxed paper under each ball.

YIELD: 7 or 8 balls

Popcorn Snowman

Edible Centerpiece

1   recipe for Popcorn balls
     listed above
8 to 10 raisins

1   chocolate cookie
1   marshmallow

Shape snowman while corn is still warm. You will need 3 different size balls; 6 to 7inch for lower body, 4- to 5- inch ball for upper body and a slightly smaller one for the head. Shape arms about 2 inches by 4 inches and press at shoulders at a raised angle. Use raisins for face, chocolate cookie with marshmallow on top for hat. Children's Delight.

COOKIES

Christmas Cookie

2 sticks butter	2¼ cups flour
1 cup powdered sugar	1 cup chopped nuts
1 egg	2 cups candied cherry halves
1 teaspoon vanilla	

Cream butter and sugar. Add egg and vanilla and mix well. Gradually add flour and beat until well mixed. Add nuts and cherries. Chill dough about 1 hour. Roll into 2 or 3 rolls; wrap in waxed paper and chill for several hours. Slice and bake at 325 degrees for 12 to 15 minutes.

Old Fashioned Refrigerator Cookie

3 cups flour	1¼ cups sugar
1 teaspoon baking powder	3 eggs
¼ teaspoon salt	1 teaspoon vanilla
2 sticks margarine	½ cup chopped nuts

Sift flour, baking powder and salt together. Cream margarine and sugar. Add eggs one at a time and mix well. Add flour mixture; mix well and add vanilla and nuts. Roll in 2-inch diameter rolls. Wrap in waxed paper — refrigerate until firm. Cut, place on cookie sheet and bake at 375 degrees for 8 minutes.

Petticoat Tails

2 sticks softened butter	2½ cups sifted flour
1 cup sifted powdered sugar	¼ teaspoon salt
1 teaspoon vanilla (or almond)	

Cream butter and sugar. Add vanilla. Sift flour and salt and mix in by hand. Mold into 2 smooth rolls 2 inches in diameter. Roll in waxed paper and chill several hours or overnight. Cut into thin slices. Place on ungreased cookie sheet and bake 8 to 10 minutes at 400 degrees.

YIELD: 6 dozen 2-inch cookies

Press Cookies

Excellent for the holidays

2	sticks butter	1	egg
1¼	cups powdered sugar	2½	cups flour
1	teaspoon vanilla	¼	teaspoon salt

Sift flour with salt and set aside. Cream butter and sugar; add egg and vanilla and beat until smooth and fluffy. Stir in flour mixture, with a spoon until well mixed. Place dough in cookie press of your choice. Press onto ungreased cookie sheet and bake a 375 degrees for 8 to 10 minutes, until they just begin to lightly brown at edges a little.

These are excellent for the Holiday Season. There are so many different shapes and so many easy ways to decorate the cookies. Children will love helping make them.

CHRISTMAS TREES: Add a little green food coloring to the dough and place a red cinnamon candy on the top or use plain dough and decorate with colored sugar.

WREATH: Use green dough or plain. Add 2 or 3 red cinnamon candies around circle to look like holly.

CANDY CANES: Use a round tube press and curve in shape of cane. Ice red stripes.

Crunchy Bran Cookies

1¼	cups firmly packed brown sugar	1	cup unprocessed bran
2	sticks margarine	1	teaspoon soda
2	eggs	1	teaspoon cinnamon
1	teaspoon vanilla	½	teaspoon salt
2¼	cups flour	1	cup raisins
		½	cup chopped nuts

Beat sugar and margarine together until light and fluffy. Mix in eggs and vanilla. Stir together flour, bran, soda, cinnamon and salt. Gradually add to creamed mixture. Mix well. Stir in raisins an nuts. Drop by teaspoon onto greased cookie sheet and bake at 375 degrees 8 to 10 minutes.

YIELD: 4 dozen

Carrot Cookie

1 stick butter, softened
1 cup light brown sugar
½ cup granulated sugar
1 teaspoon vanilla
1 egg

1 cup boiled and mashed
   carrots, cooled
2 cups flour
½ teaspoon salt
1½ teaspoons baking powder
½ cup raisins

Cream butter and sugars until smooth. Add vanilla and egg. Beat well. Add carrots. Combine flour, salt and baking powder. Sift together and add to creamed mixture. Beat until smooth. Add raisins. Drop by teaspoon on greased cookie sheet 3 inches apart. Bake at 375 degrees 10 to 12 minutes.

YIELD: 3 dozen

Glazed Carrot Cookie

2 sticks margarine or butter
1 cup sugar
2 eggs
1 7½-ounce jar baby food
   carrots — junior style
1 teaspoon vanilla
1 teaspoon lemon
2¾ cups flour
1 tablespoon baking powder

GLAZE:
¼ cup orange juice
2½ to 3 cups powdered sugar

Melt butter and stir in sugar, eggs, carrots and flavoring. Mix until smooth. Combine flour and baking powder and gradually add to creamed mixture, stirring until smooth. Cover and chill for 1 hour. Drop by teaspoon on greased cookie sheet. Bake at 375 degrees for 10 to 12 minutes. For glaze combine orange juice and powdered sugar; mix until smooth but thick. Spread on cookies while still warm.

YIELD: 7 to 8 dozen

Chocolate Chip-Oatmeal Cookies

1½ cups flour
1   teaspoon soda
1   teaspoon salt
1   cup margarine
¾   cup brown sugar
¾   cup white sugar
2   eggs

1   teaspoon hot water
1   teaspoon vanilla
1   12-ounce bag chocolate morsels
1   cup chopped nuts
2   cups oatmeal

Sift four, soda and salt and set aside. Cream margarine and sugars. Add eggs one at a time, beating well. Add hot water, vanilla and then flour mixture. Mix well. Stir in chocolate drops, nuts and oatmeal. Drop on greased cookie sheet and bake at 350 degrees 10 to 12 minutes.

YIELD: 5 dozen

Cherry Chocolate Drops

1   stick butter
1½ squares unsweetened chocolate
1   cup firmly packed brown sugar
½   cup buttermilk
1   egg
1   teaspoon vanilla

2½ cups all-purpose flour
½   teaspoon baking soda
¼   teaspoon salt
1   6-ounce bag chocolate morsels
½   cup cherries, chopped

In a small saucepan over low heat, melt together butter and unsweetened chocolate. Beat in sugar, buttermilk, egg and vanilla. Stir together flour, soda and salt and gradually mix into chocolate mixture. Stir in chocolate pieces and cherries. Drop by rounded teaspoonfuls onto greased cookie sheets. Bake in preheated 375 degree oven 10 to 12 minutes. Remove from sheets to cool.

YIELD: 5 dozen

Peanutty Chocolate Cookie

1 stick margarine	1½ cups sifted flour
3 squares unsweetened chocolate	1 cup salted peanuts
1½ cups sugar	
3 eggs	

Combine margarine and chocolate in sauce pan over low heat. Stir until melted. Remove from heat and stir in sugar. Add eggs one at a time beating well after each. Stir in flour and nuts. Place dough in refrigerator for a least 2 hours. Drop by teaspoonfuls on greased cookie sheet. Bake at 350 degrees for 12 to 15 minutes.

YIELD: 4 dozen

Coconut Chews

1½ sticks margarine	1 cup flour
1 cup brown sugar	1 teaspoon baking soda
1 egg	¾ cup flaked coconut
1 teaspoon vanilla	
1½ cups graham cracker crumbs	

Melt margarine. Add sugar, egg, vanilla, and crumbs; stir until smooth. Mix flour and soda together. Gradually add flour mixture and stir until smooth. Mix in coconut. Cover and chill at least 1 hour. Drop by teaspoonfuls on greased cookie sheet. Bake at 350 degrees 8 to 12 minutes.

YIELD: 6 dozen

Fruit Cake Cookie

Excellent with or without spirit

1   16-ounce package candied cherries, chopped
1   16-ounce package green candied pineapple, chopped
3   cups chopped nuts
2   cups raisins
3   cups flour, divided
1   teaspoon baking soda
¼   teaspoon salt
1   teaspoon cinnamon
1   teaspoon nutmeg
1   teaspoon ground cloves
1   stick margarine
1   cup firmly packed brown sugar
4   eggs
½   cup bourbon (optional)
3   tablespoons milk

Mix ½ cup flour with cherries, pineapple, nuts, and raisins. Toss to coat. Combine 2½ cups flour, soda, salt cinnamon, nutmeg and cloves; set aside. Soften margarine and beat in sugar. Continue beating until light and fluffy. Add eggs and mix well. Add flour mixture gradually. Add milk and bourbon if desired. Stir in fruit mixture. Drop by teaspoonfuls on lightly greased cookie sheet. Bake 300 degrees for 20 minutes.

YIELD: 9 dozen

Forgotten Cookies

2   egg whites
½   teaspoon cream of tartar
Pinch of salt
⅔   cup sugar
1   teaspoon vanilla
½   cup chocolate morsels
½   cup chopped nuts

Beat egg whites until foamy; add cream of tartar and salt. Beat in sugar, until sugar dissolves and whites are stiff. Fold in vanilla, chocolate drops, and nuts. Drop by teaspoon on greased cookie sheet. (Cookies will not spread.) Place cookies in oven preheated to 400 degrees. Immediately turn off oven and "forget cookies" until morning or at least 4 hours.

Ginger Cookie

1½ sticks margarine
1 cup sugar
1 egg
¼ cup molasses
2 cups flour

1½ teaspoons baking soda
¼ teaspoon salt
2 teaspoons ginger
½ teaspoon cinnamon

Beat margarine and sugar; add egg and molasses. Sift together flour, soda, salt, ginger and cinnamon; add to mixture and beat until smooth. Roll into small 1 inch balls and place on ungreased cookie sheet; press out with fork. Bake for 10 minutes at 350 degrees. Remove from oven and let cool on pan for one minute. Place on paper towel or rack to cool and become firm.

YIELD: 3½dozen

Lemon Whippersnaps

1 2-layer lemon cake mix
2 cups (4½ ounces) frozen whipped topping

1 egg
½ cup powdered sugar

Combine dry cake mix, thawed topping and egg. Stir until well mixed. Drop by teaspoonfuls into powdered sugar. Roll in sugar to coat. Place on greased cookie sheet 2 inches apart. Bake 350 degrees for 10 to 15 minutes.

YIELD: 48

Oatmeal Cookie

1 stick margarine
1 cup sugar
1 egg
3 tablespoons sour cream or 3 tablespoons milk mixed with 1 teaspoon vinegar

1½ cups flour
1 teaspoon cinnamon
½ teaspoon soda
½ teaspoon salt
1¼ cups rolled oats

Cream margarine and sugar. Add egg and sour cream or milk. Combine flour, cinnamon, soda and salt. Add to creamed mixture. Add oatmeal. Drop by spoonfuls on greased cookie sheet. Bake at 350 degrees for 10 to 15 minutes.

Peanut Butter Cookie

2	sticks margarine or butter	2	eggs
1	cup creamy peanut butter	3	cups flour
1	cup granulated sugar	1	teaspoon soda
1	cup brown sugar		

Melt margarine and peanut butter. Stir in sugars and eggs; mix well. Mix flour and soda and stir into peanut butter mixture. Stir until smooth. Chill 1 hour. Drop by teaspoonfuls onto greased cookie sheet. Flatten cookies with fork to make cross design. Bake at 350 degrees for 8 to 12 minutes.

YIELD: 8 dozen

Peanut Butter Kisses

1	cup creamy peanut butter	½	teaspoon baking powder
1½	sticks margarine	¼	teaspoon salt
½	cup firmly packed dark brown sugar		About 48 milk chocolate candies (chocolate kisses or silver bells)
2	eggs		
2½	cups flour		

Beat peanut butter, margarine and sugar. Add eggs. combine flour, baking powder and salt. Add to mixture. Beat at low speed until well blended. Roll dough into ball; wrap with plastic wrap and refrigerate until easy to handle (about 1 hour). Shape dough into balls; place 2 inches apart on ungreased cookie sheet. Press top and flatten with fork. Bake at 375 degrees for 15 minutes or until golden. Remove from oven and quickly press a candy into center of each cookie.

YIELD: 4 dozen

Pecan Party Cookie

2 sticks butter or margarine
1 cup sugar
2 eggs, separated
1 teaspoon vanilla

2 cups flour
¼ teaspoon salt
2½ cups finely chopped pecans

Cream butter and sugar. Add egg yolks and vanilla. Combine flour and salt; add to creamed mixture. Chill dough in refrigerator for at least 1 hour. Pinch off dough and form into small ball. Dip each ball into slightly beaten egg whites and then roll in nuts. Place on ungreased baking sheet and press thumb into center. Bake at 350 degrees 15 to 18 minutes.

Pumpkin Delights

⅓ cup margarine
1½ cups firmly packed light
    brown sugar
3 eggs
1 cup canned pumpkin
½ teaspoon orange extract

2½ cups self-rising flour
1 teaspoon cinnamon
¼ teaspoon ginger
¼ teaspoon nutmeg
¼ teaspoon allspice
1 cup chopped pecans

Cream margarine and sugar until light and fluffy. Add eggs one at a time, mix well after each addition. Add pumpkin and orange flavoring; blend well. Stir together flour, cinnamon, ginger, nutmeg, and allspice; add to creamed mixture. Stir in nuts. Drop by tablespoonfuls onto greased cookie sheet. Bake at 400 degrees 12 to 15 minutes.

Snowballs

½ pound butter
5 tablespoons sugar
½ teaspoon salt

2 cups flour
1 cup finely chopped pecans
Powdered sugar

Soften butter, add sugar and mix well. Add salt, flour and nuts. Roll into small balls. Bake at 325 degrees. Roll in powdered sugar.

Rolled Butter Cookie

Cookie Cutter Delights

2	sticks butter	3	cups all-purpose flour
1	cup sugar	½	teaspoon baking powder
1	egg	½	teaspoon salt
2	tablespoons milk		Red and green colored sugar
1	teaspoon vanilla		crystals. optional

Beat together butter and sugar until light and fluffy. Blend in egg, milk and vanilla. Combine flour, baking powder, and salt; add to butter mixture, mixing until well blended. Roll out on lightly floured surface ⅛-inch thick; cut with floured cookie cutters. Sprinkle with red and green colored sugar crystals if desired. Bake on ungreased cookie sheet in 350 degree oven. For 3-inch cookies bake 8 to 10 minutes or until edges are lightly browned.

YIELD: 5 dozen

Scotch Shortbread

2	sticks margarine or butter	2	cups flour
½	cup powdered sugar		

Cream butter; gradually add sugar. Combine flour and stir into creamed mixture. Roll on lightly floured surface ¼ inch thick. Cut, place on cookie sheet and prick tops with fork. Bake at 350 degrees for 20 to 25 minutes.

YIELD: 30 cookies

Gingerbread Boys and Girls

COOKIE DOUGH
3½ cups flour
1 teaspoon baking soda
¼ teaspoon salt
1½ teaspoons ground ginger
1 teaspoon ground cloves
½ cup butter or margarine, softened
¾ cup light-brown sugar, packed
1 egg

¾ cup light molasses
Optional decorations, raisins, candied cherries
FROSTING:
3 egg whites
1 1-pound box powdered sugar

Dough must be made a day ahead and refrigerated overnight. Combine flour, soda, salt, ginger and cloves and set aside. Cream butter and sugar in mixer. Add eggs and beat until light and fluffy. Add molasses and beat until blended. Add flour mixture gradually and mix with spoon and hands until dough is well blended. Divide dough in 4 parts — wrap each tightly and refrigerate overnight.

Work one piece of dough at a time leaving others in refrigerator to remain firm. Roll dough on a lightly floured surface to ⅛ inch thickness. Cut out gingerbread men, place on lightly greased cookie sheet about 1 inch apart. If you are not going to frost cookies, place ½ raisins for eyes and buttons. Cut sliver of candied cherry for mouth. Bake in a 375 degree preheated oven 6 to 8 minutes or until lightly browned. Remove to wire rack to cool.

FROSTING: Beat egg whites and powdered sugar until smooth and stiff. Place in pastry bag and outline cookie with the line of frosting. Store in covered tins.

YIELD: 7 to 10 dozen depending on cookie size.

Butter Rum Cheese Bars

1	roll refrigerator slice and bake butterscotch cookies	16	ounces cream cheese
1	cup sugar	2	eggs
		2	teaspoons rum flavoring

Slice cookie dough ¼ inch thick and place in bottom of 2 greased 8 × 8-inch pans. Bake at 375 degrees for 15 to 20 minutes or until lightly browned. (Will be puffy when removed from oven.) Beat cream cheese and sugar until well mixed. Add eggs and flavoring. Beat until smooth. Pour cheese mixture over baked cookie layer. Bake at 375 degrees 20 to 25 minutes. Cool slightly, then refrigerate at least one hour. Cut into 20 bars per pan.

YIELD: 40

Butterscotch Brownies

1	stick butter or margarine	¼	teaspoon soda
2	cups brown sugar, packed	½	teaspoon salt
2	eggs	½	cup chopped pecans
1	teaspoon vanilla	1	6-ounce package semisweet butterscotch morsels
2	cups flour		
1	teaspoon baking powder		

Cream margarine and sugar until light and fluffy. Add eggs one at a time, beating well after each. Add vanilla. Combine flour, baking powder, soda and salt; add to creamed mixture, mixing until smooth. Pour into greased 13 × 9-inch pan. Sprinkle pecans and butterscotch chips over top. Bake at 350 degrees for 30 to 35 minutes. Cut into bars while warm.

YIELD: 36

Cinnamon Sticks

1½ sticks margarine
1 cup sugar
1 egg, separated
2 cups flour

2 tablespoons cinnamon
½ teaspoon salt
1 cup chopped nuts

Mix butter and sugar together with a spoon. Add egg yolk and stir well. Sift flour, cinnamon and salt together. Add to creamed mixture. Mix well and knead with hands. Pat out on cookie sheet or oblong cake pan. Beat egg white slightly and spread over dough. Sprinkle nuts over top and press lightly into dough. Bake at 325 degrees for 30 minutes. While still warm cut into squares or oblong strips.

Congo Squares

⅔ cup margarine
2¼ cups brown sugar
3 eggs
2¾ cups sifted flour

2½ teaspoons baking powder
½ teaspoon salt
1 cup chopped pecans
1 6-ounce package chocolate morsels

Melt margarine and add brown sugar. Stir until well blended. Cool slightly. Add eggs, one at a time, mixing well after each addition. Combine flour, salt and baking powder; sift together. Add to egg mixture and mix well. Add nuts and chocolate and pour into a greased 9 × 13-inch pan. Bake at 350 degrees for 45 to 50 minutes. When almost cool, cut into squares.

Luscious Lemon Bars

2	sticks margarine	2	cups sugar
½	cup powdered sugar	½	teaspoon baking powder
2½	cups flour, divided	6	tablespoons lemon juice
4	eggs		

Melt margarine and mix with sugar and 2 cups flour. Press into 9 × 13-inch pan and bake 15 to 20 minutes at 350 degrees. While baking prepare lemon layer. Beat eggs until fluffy. Add sugar and mix well. Add ½ cup flour, baking powder, and lemon juice and mix until blended. Pour over cookie layer and return to 350 degree oven for 25 minutes or until set. Cool and cut into squares.

Pecan Pie Bars

Excellent

1	2-layer yellow cake mix	1½	cups corn syrup
½	stick margarine, melted	1	teaspoon vanilla
4	eggs	1	cup chopped pecans
½	cup brown sugar		

Measure ⅔ cup cake mix and set aside. Combine remaining cake mix, melted margarine and one egg. Mix until crumbly. Press in bottom of greased 13 × 9 × 2-inch pan. Bake until light brown, 15 to 20 minutes. While crust is baking combine the remaining cake mix with sugar, syrup, vanilla and 3 eggs. Beat until well blended. Remove crust from oven. Pour filling over top and sprinkle with chopped nuts. Return to 350 degree oven and bake for 30 to 35 minutes. Cool and cut into bars.

6 Layer Cookies

1   stick butter or margarine
1½ cups graham cracker
     crumbs
1   can flaked coconut
1   cup chopped pecans

1   12-ounce package of
     chocolate chips
1   14-ounce can condensed
     milk

Melt margarine in $13 \times 9 \times 2$-inch pan or baking dish. Sprinkle graham cracker crumbs evenly in bottom of pan. Follow with layer of coconut, chocolate chips and nuts. Pat down each layer. Top with condensed milk. With back of spoon pack the mixture down. Let this stand for a few minutes so the milk can be absorbed in the layers. Bake at 350 degrees for 25 minutes (or until nuts just begin to brown). Cool before cutting in bars. (Cuts better if put in refrigerator.)

Buttered Pecan Turtle Cookies

CRUST:
2   cups all purpose flour
1   cup brown sugar, packed
½   cup butter or margarine
1   cup pecan halves

FILLING:
⅔   cup butter or margarine
½   cup brown sugar, packed

TOPPING:
1   cup chocolate chips

Preheat oven 350 degrees. In large bowl combine flour, sugar, and margarine. Mix well until particles are fine. Pat firmly into ungreased $13 \times 9 \times 2$-inch pan. Sprinkle pecans over unbaked crust. To prepare carmel layer combine butter and sugar in heavy sauce pan. Cook over medium heat stirring constantly until entire surface begins to boil. Boil 1 minute longer. Pour over unbaked crust and pecans. Bake 18 to 20 minutes or until entire caramel layer is bubbly. Remove from oven and immediately sprinkle with milk chocolate chips. Allow chips to melt slightly (2 to 3 minutes). Swirl chips slightly to give marbled effect. Cool, cut.

YIELD: 3 to 4 dozen.

Creamy Cheese Squares

1	yellow cake mix, 2-layer size	1	cup chopped nuts
1	stick butter or margarine	1	1-pound box powdered sugar
3	eggs	8	ounces cream cheese

Melt butter and stir into cake mix. Add one egg and nuts. Mixture will be crumbly. Press into greased 13 × 9-inch cake pan. Beat softened cream cheese, powdered sugar and 2 eggs until creamy. Pour over layer in pan and bake at 350 degrees for 30 to 40 minutes. Cut into bars. Very rich.

YIELD: 24

Rocky Road Squares

½	cup butter or margarine	2	cups miniature marshmallows
½	cup brown sugar	1	6-ounce semi sweet chocolate morsels
1	cup flour	½	cup chopped nuts
½	cup graham cracker crust		

Combine butter and sugar and beat until light and fluffy. Mix flour and cracker crumbs together and add to creamed mixture. Pat into greased 9 × 9-inch cake pan. Spread marshmallows, chocolate, and nuts on top of crust. Bake at 375 degrees for 15 to 20 minutes. Cool and cut into squares.

PIES

Chocolate Bourbon Pie

1 stick butter, melted
1 cup sugar
1 cup light corn syrup
4 eggs, beaten
1 to 3 tablespoons bourbon, optional

1 6-ounce bag chocolate morsels
1 cup chopped pecans
1 unbaked 9-inch pie shell
Whipped cream or frozen topping

Combine all ingredients except whipped cream. Mix well and pour into pie shell. Bake at 350 degrees for 40 to 45 minutes or until firm. Serve warm with whipped cream.

YIELD: 1 pie

Chocolate Chip Pie

1 6-ounce package chocolate morsels
3 tablespoons milk
3 tablespoons sugar

4 eggs, divided
1 teaspoon vanilla
Whipped cream
1 baked pie shell

Melt chocolate morsels over hot water and blend with milk and sugar. Cool. Add egg yolks and vanilla and beat well. Add stiffly beaten egg white, folding carefully into chocolate mixture. Spoon into baked pie shell. Chill several hours. Top with sweetened whipped cream.

SERVES: 6

Hershey Bar Pie

Super, delicious and easy

1 graham cracker pie shell	18 to 24 marshmallows
6 Hershey bars with almonds (1.35 ounce size)	½ cup milk
	½ 9-ounce tub whipped frozen topping

Place milk, candy bars, and marshmallows in top of double boiler and melt. When melted set out of water and cool completely. Fold frozen topping into the chocolate. Pour into pie crust and chill in refrigerator for at least 3 hours or until ready to serve.

Coconut Pie

⅓ cup flour	1 teaspoon vanilla
⅔ cup sugar	1 cup fresh coconut or 6
¼ teaspoon salt	ounces frozen
2 cups milk	1 cup whipped cream or Cool
3 egg yolks	Whip
2 tablespoons butter	1 9-inch baked pie shell

Combine flour, sugar, and salt in double boiler. Scald milk and add to mixture. Beat egg yolks slightly and add a small amount of milk mixture. Slowly add the rest of milk to eggs and return to double boiler. Cook covered 2 minutes, cool and add butter, vanilla, and coconut. Pour into shell and top with slightly sweetened whipped cream.

Coconut Chiffon Pie

2 recipes make 3 big pies

4	eggs, separated
¼	teaspoon salt
1	cup sugar, divided
1½	cups milk
1	envelope plain gelatin

1	teaspoon vanilla
6	ounces frozen coconut
1	baked pie shell
	Whipped cream-topping

Beat egg yolks. Combine yolks, salt, ½ cup sugar, milk, and gelatin in top of double boiler. Cook until begins to thicken. Cool until mushy; add vanilla and coconut. Beat egg whites with remaining ½ cup sugar; fold in pie. Pour into cool pie shell. Top with whipped cream.

Impossible Pie

½	cup Bisquick
½	cup sugar
4	eggs
2	cups milk

1	4-ounce can coconut
1	teaspoon vanilla
3	tablespoons butter

Put everything in a blender. Mix well. Pour into a well buttered 10-inch pie plate. Bake until custard sets. 400 degree oven for 25 to 30 minutes.

Pecan Chiffon Pie

A real treat

4   eggs, separated
¼   teaspoon salt
1   cup sugar, divided
1   cup milk
1   envelope plain gelatin
¼   cup cold water

1   teaspoon vanilla
1   cup chopped pecans, toasted
1   9-inch pie shell, baked
1   cup cream, whipped and sweetened

Beat egg yolks and place in sauce pan with salt and ½ cup sugar. In separate sauce pan heat milk and pour over egg mixture. Cook over low heat; bring to a boil and cook until thickens. Remove from heat. Dissolve gelatin in water and add at once to hot mixture. Add vanilla and set custard aside to cool completely. Beat egg whites until stiff, adding remaining ½ cup sugar. Fold into cooled custard. Gradually fold in nuts. Spoon into baked pie shell and refrigerate. After pie is firm top with sweetened whipped cream. Spread on top of pie — refrigerate until serving.

Southern Pecan Pie

3   eggs, beaten
¾   cup sugar
¾   cup light corn syrup
1   teaspoon vanilla

1   cup chopped pecans
3   tablespoons butter, melted
1   9-inch pie shell

Mix slightly beaten eggs, sugar, syrup and vanilla. Pour into pie shell. Sprinkle nuts on top and pat down. Pour melted butter over nuts. Bake at 325 degrees for 1 hour or until mixture is set.

Pumpkin Pie

2	eggs (slightly beaten)	½	teaspoon ginger
1	1-pound can pumpkin	¼	teaspoon cloves
¾	cup sugar	1	13-ounce can evaporated
½	teaspoon salt		milk
1	teaspoon cinnamon	1	9-inch unbaked pie crust

Beat egg just until mixed. Add pumpkin, sugar, salt, cinnamon, ginger, and cloves. Add milk. Pour into pie shell and bake in a hot 425 degree oven for 15 minutes. Reduce temperature to 350 degrees and continue baking for 45 minutes or until knife inserted in center comes out clean.

Pumpkin Pecan Pie

1	unbaked pie shell	1	cup sugar
¼	cup brown sugar	1	cup milk
3	tablespoons butter	2	cups pumpkin
½	cup chopped pecans	½	teaspoon salt
FILLING		½	teaspoon cinnamon
2	eggs	½	teaspoon nutmeg

Mix sugar, softened butter and pecans; press into unbaked pie crust. Bake at 350 degrees for 3 to 5 minutes, remove from oven. Beat eggs well. Mix in sugar, milk, pumpkin, salt, cinnamon and nutmeg. Pour into pie shell and bake at 425 degrees for 15 minutes. Turn temperature down to 350 degrees and bake for 45 minutes.

Pumpkin Mincemeat Pie

1	unbaked pie crust	1	egg
2	cups mincemeat	2	teaspoons pumpkin pie
¾	cup pumpkin		spice
⅓	cup firmly packed brown	1	5½-ounce can evaporated
	sugar		milk (⅔ cup)

Spread mincemeat in bottom of unbaked pie crust. Combine pumpkin, sugar, egg, and pie spice. Gradually add milk, mixing well. Pour over mincemeat. Bake in a preheated 375 degree oven 50 to 55 minutes. Test by inserting knife in center.

Apple Pie

½ cup sugar
¼ cup brown sugar
2 tablespoons flour
¼ teaspoon salt
½ teaspoon cinnamon
¼ teaspoon nutmeg
2 tablespoons butter
Apples to fill shell or 1 can of
    pie sliced apples
Dough for 2 crusts

Combine and mix sugars, flour, salt, cinnamon, and nutmeg. Place sliced apples in unbaked shell, pour dry mixture over apples. Place pats of butter on top and cover with top layer of dough. Make several slits in dough. Bake at 350 degrees for 30 to 40 minutes.

Ozark Apple Pie

1 egg
¾ cup sugar
½ cup flour
1¼ teaspoons baking powder
⅛ teaspoon salt
½ cup chopped nuts
½ cup peeled, chopped apples
½ teaspoon vanilla
Whipping cream
3 tablespoons applesauce
¼ teaspoon cinnamon
Sugar

Beat egg and sugar together. Combine and sift the flour, baking powder, and salt; add to first mixture. Add nuts, apples, and vanilla. Pour into a buttered 9-inch pie plate and bake at 350 degrees for 35 minutes. Whip cream, add a little sugar, and when thickened, add applesauce and cinnamon. Serve over pie.

Speedy Cheese Pie

1½ cups graham cracker
crumbs
¼ cup butter, melted
8 ounces cream cheese
1 tablespoon lemon juice
½ teaspoon vanilla
½ cup sugar
2 eggs

TOPPING:
1 cup sour cream
2 tablespoons butter
½ teaspoon vanilla
1 21-ounce can pie filling
(optional) blueberry, cherry
or strawberry

Combine crumbs and melted butter and pat into 8-inch pie plate. Beat cheese until fluffy while adding sugar, lemon and vanilla. Add eggs one at a time beating thoroughly after each addition. Pour into crumb crust and bake 25 to 30 minutes in 325 degree oven or until set. Combine sour cream, butter, and vanilla. Spoon over top of pie. Bake 10 minutes longer. Cool. Chill several hours before serving. If glaze desired, chill can; just before serving spoon over pie slices.

Coconut Cheese Pie

2 tablespoons margarine
3 cups flake coconut
4 eggs

⅔ cup sugar
8 ounces cream cheese
3 tablespoons lemon juice

Spread softened margarine on sides and bottom of a 9-inch pie pan. Press 1½ cups of coconut on sides and bottom into margarine to form a coconut pie shell. Combine eggs, sugar, cream cheese, lemon juice and 1 cup of coconut in blender. Blend until smooth and pour into coconut pie shell. Lay remaining ½ cup of coconut around edge to form top of crust. Place in a 325 degree oven and bake for 30 minutes. Watch; if coconut on top edge begins to brown cover with aluminum foil.

Strawberry Pie

2   cups fresh strawberries,
    sliced
½   cup sugar
2   tablespoons cornstarch
1½ cups water

½   teaspoon salt
1   3-ounce package strawberry
    flavored gelatin
1   baked pie crust
Frozen whipped topping mix

Mix sugar, cornstarch, salt and water in sauce pan. Cook until thickens and clears slightly. Add strawberry gelatin and stir until dissolved. Set aside until thickens slightly. Place layer of gelatin mixture over bottom of pie crust. Place berries on mixture. Pour remaining mixture over, sealing in berries. Refrigerate at least two hours before serving. Put small amount of frozen topping mix on each slice.

SERVES: 6

Yogurt Pie

1   graham cracker crust
1   4-ounce package cream
    cheese

2   cartons yogurt (any flavor)
1   9-ounce carton frozen
    whipped topping

Soften cream cheese. Blend with yogurt. Fold in topping mix. Pour into shell and refrigerate.

Peanut Butter Pie

1 8-ounce package cream
   cheese
¾ cup powdered sugar
¾ cup chunky peanut butter
6 tablespoons milk

½ teaspoon vanilla
1 9-ounce carton frozen
   whipped topping
1 graham cracker pie crust

Combine cream cheese, powdered sugar, peanut butter and milk. Beat at medium speed until well blended, 3 to 4 minutes. Add vanilla. Fold in topping mix. Spoon into graham cracker crust. For a festive look you can sprinkle peanuts or grated chocolate on top with a few dollops of topping. Refrigerate pie at least 4 hours before serving.

Egg Custard Pie

Easy

1 pie shell
3 eggs
2 cups milk

½ teaspoon vanilla
½ cup sugar
Pinch of salt

Beat eggs just until mixed. Add sugar and stir well. Add milk, vanilla and salt; beat lightly. Pour into unbaked pie shell. Bake on bottom shelf of oven at 350 degrees for 10 minutes. Move to center of oven, reduce heat to 325 degrees and bake for 30 to 40 minutes longer or until done.

Busy Days Pies

Lemon, Key Lime, Pineapple

1   graham cracker pie shell
1   15-ounce can condensed
     milk
1   9-ounce carton non-dairy
     frozen topping
FLAVOR OF YOUR CHOICE
1   (6-ounce) can frozen
     lemonade or

1   (6-ounce) can frozen
     Limeade or
1   (20-ounce) can crushed
     pineapple and ⅓ cup lemon
     juice
Green or yellow food coloring

Mix condensed milk and softened non-dairy frozen topping mix. Add thawed frozen limeade for Key Lime pie, frozen lemonade for lemon pie, or 20-ounce can crushed pineapple, drained and ⅓ cup lemon juice for pineapple pie. Add one or two drops of coloring, green for key lime or yellow for others. Stir together until smooth. Pour into pie shell. Chill several hours before serving. Doubled recipe makes 3 pies.

 # BEVERAGES

Hot Buttered Rum

2	sticks butter	1	pint vanilla ice cream, softened
1	pound brown sugar		Light Rum
1	teaspoons cinnamon		Whipped cream or topping
1	teaspoons nutmeg		Cinnamon stick, optional

Set ice cream out to soften. Combine softened butter, sugar, cinnamon and nutmeg. Beat until light and fluffy. Spoon in ice cream and stir until well mixed. Place in freezer containers and freeze. At serving time thaw slightly. Place 2 to 3 tablespoons of butter mixture in mug. Add 1 jigger of rum; fill with boiling water and stir. Serve with cinnamon stick and dollop of whipped cream. Recipe can easily be cut for smaller quantities.

YIELD: 10 to 12 cups

Holiday Mull

1	1½-quart bottle Cranberry juice	½	teaspoon salt
2	1-quart bottles apple juice	4	cinnamon sticks
½	cup brown sugar	1½	teaspoons whole cloves

Combine cranberry juice, apple juice, brown sugar and salt in electric slow cooker or large sauce pan. Stir until sugar is dissolved. Tie cinnamon sticks and cloves in cheese cloth and place in liquid. Cover pot and cook for 2 hours on low. Do not boil. Electric slow-cooker or crockpot works great. Remove spices and serve.

YIELD: 28 4-ounce servings

Hot Wine

1	quart of dry red wine	½	cup sugar
2	cups orange juice	4	whole cloves
½	cup lemon juice	1	cinnamon stick

Combine all the ingredients and heat until sugar dissolves. Remove cloves and cinnamon stick. Serve hot.

YIELD: 7 cups

Coffee Punch Royal

½-ounce jar instant coffee		1	cup carbonated water
2	cups boiling water	1	cup brandy
2	cups sugar	1	cup bourbon
2	quarts light cream	1	pint heavy cream, whipped

Dissolve coffee and sugar in boiling water. Chill. Place a block of ice in punch bowl. Pour chilled liquid, light cream, carbonated water, brandy and bourbon over ice. Top with whipped cream. Makes 4½ quarts or 36½ cup servings.

Egg Nog

6	eggs, separated	1½	cups bourbon
¾	cup sugar, divided	2	tablespoon dark rum
2	cups milk		Nutmeg
2	cups heavy cream		

Beat egg yolks well. Add ½ cup sugar and continue to beat until sugar dissolves. Add milk and cream, then slowly add bourbon and rum. Refrigerate 3 to 4 hours. When ready to serve beat egg whites until stiff. Gradually beat in ¼ cup sugar; fold into mixture. Sprinkle lightly with nutmeg.

Very Good Punch

1	3½-ounce package lime gelatin	2	cups sugar
1	3½-ounce package lemon gelatin	1	large can pineapple juice
		2	lemons
2	cups water	32	ounce gingerale

Dissolve flavored gelatin in 2 cups boiling water. Add sugar and stir to dissolve. Add pineapple juice, juice of 2 lemons and enough water to make 1 gallon. Just before serving add 1 quart of gingerale.

Lime Julip

1	cup lime juice	4	cups unsweetened pineapple juice
1	cup sugar	1	quart gingerale

Combine lime juice and sugar in sauce pan. Heat until sugar is dissolved. Add pineapple juice, stir well and set off heat to cool. At serving time add gingerale and pour over crushed ice. Serve with a slice of lime on glass.

YIELD: 12 servings

Mocha Punch

1	ounce chocolate	½	cup heavy cream
¼	cup sugar	1	teaspoon vanilla
⅛	teaspoon salt	2	cups strong chilled coffee
1¾	cups boiling water		Vanilla Ice Cream
½	cup milk		

Melt chocolate over hot water. Add sugar, salt, and boiling water to melted chocolate. Stir and cook for 5 minutes. Add milk, heavy cream and chill. Mix vanilla with strong coffee and add to first mixture. Beat well. Serve in chilled glasses with scoop of vanilla ice cream in each. Makes 5 cups.

Hot Chocolate Mix

Great for youngsters — no mess

1   2-pound box Nestles Quick
1   8-quart box powdered milk

1   8 to 11-ounce jar powdered
    coffee cream
1   box powdered sugar

In large bowl combine all ingredients and mix well. Store in tight container. Place 4 or 5 spoonfuls in cup and add boiling water. This is great for every age — no milk to heat — no mess. This makes enough for your family and several jars for gifts.

Instant Spiced Tea

¾   cup instant tea with lemon
1   27-ounce jar orange Tang
2   cups sugar

1   teaspoon cloves
2   teaspoons ground
    cinnamon

Combine and mix all ingredients well. Keep in a tightly-covered jar. To serve: Mix 2 teaspoons mixture in 1 cup of boiling water.

Coffee Liqueur

Homemade Kahlua

3½ cups sugar
⅓   cup instant coffee
2   cups water

1   fifth vodka
3   tablespoon plus 1 teaspoon
    vanilla

Combine coffee, sugar and water. Heat until dissolved; cool. Add vodka and vanilla. Pour into half gallon glass container. Age two weeks. Use as is for Kahlua or serve mixed with milk.

POTPOURRI

Cranberry Jelly

1 quart cranberry juice cocktail	4 cups sugar
1 6-ounce bottle Certo	¼ cup lemon juice

Combine cranberry juice and Certo in a large heavy sauce pan. Cook over high heat, stirring constantly, until mixture comes to a rolling boil. Stir in sugar and return to a boil. Boil 2 minutes, stirring constantly. Remove from heat; add lemon juice. Skim off foam and pour into sterilized jars. Seal at once.

Cranberry Conserve

1 pound cranberries	2 cups sugar
1 cup water	½ cup raising
1 orange, ground	½ cup chopped nuts

Cook berries and water until berries pop open. Mash berries; then add ground orange, sugar, and raisins. Cook until thickens (2 drops of syrup run together from side of spoon). Remove from heat and stir in nuts. Pour into sterilized jars immediately and seal.

Mint Jelly

1 cup water	½ cup vinegar
2 cups fresh mint, leaves and stems	3 ounces Certo
	Green food coloring
3½ cups sugar	

Combine water, mint, sugar, and vingar in heavy pan. Bring to a rolling boil. Add Certo, return to a boil for 3 to 3½ minutes. Strain through several layers of cheese cloth. Add touch of green coloring. Pour into sterilized jars and seal or cover with paraffin. Baby food jars make clever gift size containers.

YIELD: 5 to 7 jars

Jalapeño Jelly

4   large bell peppers
12   jalapeño peppers
1½ cups cider vinegar

6½ cups sugar
1   6-ounce bottle of Certo
Few drops green food coloring

Remove seeds and cut peppers into small pieces. Add vinegar and sugar, boil for 10 minutes. Strain through cheese cloth. Add red or green food coloring. Bring to a boil and add Certo. Boil 1 minute, remove from heat and skim. Pour into sterilized contaners and cover with paraffin. Peppers can be chopped in blender by adding a little of vinegar.

YIELD: 6 half pint jars

Wine Jelly

Makes a great gift

2   cups Burgandy or Rosé
3   cups sugar

3   ounces of Certo

Place wine and sugar in top of double boiler. Cook over simmering heat until sugar is dissolved. Remove from heat and add 3 ounces of Certo (6 tablespoons). Pour into sterilized jars and seal.

YIELD: 5 8-ounce jars

Candy Mint Nuts

1   cup sugar
1   tablespoon light corn syrup
¼   cup water
6   marshmallows (quartered)

¼   teaspoon essence of
     peppermint
3   cups pecans

Boil sugar, syrup, and water for 1 minute. Add marshmallows and peppermint. When all is dissolved, add nuts. Turn out on waxed paper.

Sugared Pecans

⅓	cup margarine	¼	teaspoon ginger
¼	cup sugar	¼	teaspoon nutmeg
½	teaspoon cinnamon	1	pound pecan halves

Melt margarine, stir in sugar and spices. Mix well. Pour over nuts in large flat pan and mix to coat. Bake at 275 degrees for 30 minutes. Stir every 10 minutes. Store in a tight tin.

Cocktail Spiced Pecans

6	tablespoons butter	1	clove garlic, minced
½	teaspooon Tabasco sauce	1	pound shelled pecans
1	teaspoon Worcestershire		

Preheat oven to 325 degrees. Melt butter and add sauces and garlic. Heat briefly. Scatter pecans in one layer and stir to cover nuts with mixture. Bake 20 to 30 minutes, stirring often.

Swedish Nuts

1	pound shelled pecans	Dash salt	
2	egg whites	½ cup margarine	
1	cup sugar		

Toast pecans in a 325 degree oven until light brown. Beat egg whites until stiff. Fold sugar and salt into whites and beat until stiff peaks form. Fold nuts into meringue. Melt margarine in a 15 × 10-inch pan. Spread nut mixture over melted margarine and bake at 325 degrees stirring every 10 minutes. Bake about 30 minutes or until nuts are coated with light brown meringue and no margarine is left in pan. Cool.

YIELD: about 4 cups

Munchies

Easy gift

6	cups popped corn	1	stick margarine
1	6-ounce bag corn chips	2	teaspoons Worcestershire
2	cups bite-size pretzels	¼	teaspoon Tabasco
1	3-ounce can chinese noodles	⅛	teaspoon garlic powder

Combine corn, chips, pretzels and noodles. Melt margarine, stir in sauces and garlic. Pour over corn, toss to coat. Bake at 250 degrees for 1 hour. Stir every 15 minutes. Cool and store in airtight containers.

YIELD: 12 cups

Traditional Party Mix

1	stick margarine	2½	cups Wheat Chex Cereal
1¼	teaspoon seasoned salt	2½	cups Corn Chex Cereal
5	teaspoons Worcestershire sauce	1	cup salted mixed nuts
2½	cups Rice Chex Cereal		

Melt margarine in a 15 × 10-inch pan; stir in salt and Worcestershire. Add cereals and nuts carefully mixing until all pieces are coated. Heat in 250 degree oven 1 hour. Stir every 15 minutes. Cool on paper towels to drain.

Granola

5	cups rolled oats	½ to ¾	cup vegetable oil
1	cup sunflower seeds	¾ to 1	cup honey or cane syrup
½	cup sesame seeds	1	2½-ounce bag sliced almonds
½	cup wheat germ		
½	cup unprocessed Bran		

Combine all dry ingredients except almonds; mix. Pour in oil and syrup and mix well. Spread in a large flat pan and bake at 300 degrees for 50 to 60 minutes. Stir every 15 minutes and add almonds for the last 15 minutes. Cool and store in container with tight fitting lid.

Mustard with a Sass

5   tablespoons dry musard
½   cup sugar
1   tablespoon flour
Dash of red pepper

2   eggs, beaten
½   cup vinegar
1   tablespoon butter or
    margarine

Combine mustard, sugar, flour and red pepper in top of double boiler. Add beaten eggs and vinegar, blending thoroughly. Place over boiling water; cook, stirring constantly until thickened. Add butter, stir until melted. Cool mixture. Store in covered jar in refrigerator.

YIELD: 1⅓ cups

Delightful Mayonnaise

1   egg
2   cups vegetable oil
1   teaspoon salt

1   teaspoon sugar
1   tablespoon lemon juice
1   tablespoon hot water

Chill oil and lemon juice. Beat egg well in mixer or blender. While continuing to beat, slowly add oil, using a thin, slow stream. Beat in salt, sugar, water, and lemon juice.

APPETIZERS

Cheese Wafers

2 cups grated sharp cheese
2 cups flour
2 stick soft butter
2 cups Rice Krispies

¼ teaspoon red pepper
½ teaspoon paprika
½ teaspoon salt

Mix all together; form into small balls. Place balls on ungreased cookie sheet and press down with a fork. Bake in 350 degree oven for 10 minutes.

YIELD: Serves 100

Cheese Straws

1 pound sharp, cheddar cheese, grated
1 stick butter or margarine

1½ cups flour
1 teaspoon salt
½ teaspoon cayenne pepper

Cream cheese with margarine. Combine flour, salt and pepper; add to cheese and mix well. Press dough through a cookie press onto flat ungreased cookie sheet. Bake at 350 degrees for 15 to 20 minutes.

Olive-Cheese Balls

1 pound sharp cheese, grated
1 cup flour
Red pepper to taste

½ teaspoon Worcestershire sauce
Large jar medium size, stuffed olives

Let cheese stand at room temperature until soft. Add flour and seasonings and mix well. Pinch off small amount — work into thin circle and press around olive. Bake on greased sheet at 40 degrees for 10 minutes.

Cheese Cut Outs

1	stick butter or margarine	1	1¼-ounce envelope dry
4	ounces cheddar cheese, grated		onion soup mix
		1	cup flour

Mix butter and cheese, then add soup mix and flour. Blend and shape into ball and chill. Roll out on floured board. Cut into desired shapes. Bake at 375 degrees for 10 minutes. Makes about 5 dozen. (If difficult to roll out, add more flour.)

Cheese Ball

1	pound mild cheddar	1	tablespoons grated onion
1	pound sharp cheddar	1	cup finely chopped nuts
2	8-ounce packages cream cheese	½	cup chopped parsley
1	teaspoon Worcestershire	1	garlic clove, crushed
			Paprika

Soften cheeses and combine. Mix well. Add onion, Worcestershire, garlic, ½ nuts and ½ parsley. Shape into ball. Wrap in paper and refrigerate overnight. One hour before serving roll ball in remaining nuts and parsley. Sprinkle with Paprika.

Pickled Shrimp

5	pounds shrimp — boiled, peeled	1	teaspoon prepared mustard
			Dash paprika
2	large onions, sliced	1	pint vinegar
1	pint vegetable oil	2	tablespoons lemon juice
1	bottle capers and juice		Dash cayenne
1	teaspoon powdered sugar		

Layer shrimp and onions in a deep flat pan or large mouth gift jars. Combine remaining ingredients and pour over shrimp and onions. Cover, place in refrigerator 24 hours before serving. Stir several times. A fantastic gift for a man.

Oyster Dip

Super!

1	3½-ounce can of smoked oysters	Worcestershire sauce
½	pint sour cream	Tabasco sauce
		Salt

Drain oysters and chop into very small pieces. Stir in sour cream. Add salt to taste. Add 1 or 2 teaspoons of Worcestershire sauce and a couple drops of Tabasco sauce — depending on how hot you like it. Mix well and place in refrigerator. Needs to be made several hours ahead for flavor. Serve with potato chips. A favorite!

Crab St. Thomas

1	stick margarine	¼	teaspoon cayenne pepper
1	cup chopped onion	¼	teaspoon Tabasco
8	ounces cream cheese	1	pound crabmeat, fresh or canned
½	teaspoon salt		
¼	teaspoon pepper		

Saute onions in margarine. Add cream cheese, salt, peppers, and Tabasco. Stir to mix well. Fold in crabmeat and heat through. Serve warm with cracker or toast points.

Smoked Salmon Ball

1	pound can salmon	¼	teaspoon Tabasco
8	ounces cream cheese	1	tablespoon horseradish
2	tablespoons grated onion	1	tablespoon liquid smoke
¼	teaspoon salt		Nuts, finely chopped
1	tablespoon lemon juice		Parsley flakes

Drain salmon and remove skin and bones. Flake and combine with cream cheese, onion, salt, lemon juice, Tabasco, horseradish, and liquid smoke. Form into a ball. Pat nuts and parsley on cheese ball until well coated. Wrap in plastic wrap and chill. Serve with crackers.

Salmon Mousse

1	envelope unflavored gelatin	1	tablespoon grated onion
¼	cup cold water	½	teaspoon Tabasco
½	cup boiling water	1	teaspoon salt
½	cup mayonnaise	1	15½-ounce can red salmon
1	tablespoon lemon juice	½	cup heavy cream, whipped

Sprinkle gelatin over cold water to soften in a large bowl, about 5 minutes. Add boiling water; stir until dissolved. Let cool 5 minutes. Add mayonnaise, lemon juice, onion, Tabasco and salt. Mix until well blended. Chill until the consistency of unbeaten egg white. Drain salmon and puree in blender. Fold into chilled gelatin mixture. Gently fold whipped cream into salmon mixture. Turn into a 4-cup mold. Refrigerate until firm, about 4 hours or overnight. Unmold and serve.

SERVES: 8

Spinach Balls

Freezes well

2	cups Pepperidge Farm herb bread crumbs	6	eggs, beaten
2	10-ounce packages frozen chopped spinach, drained	¾	cup margarine
		½	teaspoon thyme
2	large onions, chopped fine	1	tablespoon garlic salt
½	cup Parmesan cheese	1	tablespoon Accent

Combine all ingredients and mix well. Form into bite-size balls. Place on cookie sheet and bake at 350 degrees for 20 minutes. Can be frozen and rewarmed at 350 degrees. Serve on warming tray or chafing dish.

YIELD: 100 balls

Stuffed Cherry Tomato Hors D'Oeuvres

30 good-sized cherry tomatoes
4½-ounce can deviled ham
¾ cup grated Swiss cheese, divided

½ cup finely-chopped pimento-stuffed olives
1 tablespoon minced onion

Rinse and dry tomatoes. Slice off tips, scoop out pulp, and drain shells upside down on paper towels. In a small mixing bowl, stir together the deviled ham, ½ cup of cheese, olives, and onion. Spoon into tomato shells; sprinkle with the remaining cheese. Cover and refrigerate until ready to use. Best served shortly after making. Makes about 30 hors d'oeuvres.

Easy Guacamole

2 avocados
½ teaspoon garlic salt
1 tablespoon lemon juice

2 to 3 tablespoons mayonnaise

Peel avocados, remove seeds and mash with a fork. Add lemon juice, garlic salt and mayonnaise. Refrigerate until serving. Serve with chips or crackers.

Sausage Appetizers

3 cups biscuit mix
1 pound bulk hot sausage, uncooked

1 pound shredded cheddar cheese

Combine all ingredients, mix well. Shape loosely into 1-inch balls. Place on ungreased baking sheet. Bake at 350 degrees for 12 to 15 minutes. Serve hot.

INDEX

HOLIDAY FAVORITES AND
TASTE OF THE HOLIDAYS
P.O. Box 935
Waycross, Georgia 31502
(912) 285-2848

Please send me_____copies of **HOLIDAY FAVORITES,** $6.95
per copy. Georgia residents add $.42 sales tax.

Please send me_____copies of **TASTE of the HOLIDAYS,** $3.95
per copy. Georgia residents add $.24 sales tax.

Add $1.25 postage & handling for first book, only $.50 postage
& handling for each additional book.

Enclosed is my check or money order in the amount of $_____

Name_____

Address_____

City_____State_____Zip_____

- -

HOLIDAY FAVORITES AND
TASTE OF THE HOLIDAYS
P.O. Box 935
Waycross, Georgia 31502
(912) 285-2848

Please send me_____copies of **HOLIDAY FAVORITES,** $6.95
per copy. Georgia residents add $.42 sales tax.

Please send me_____copies of **TASTE of the HOLIDAYS,** $3.95
per copy. Georgia residents add $.24 sales tax.

Add $1.25 postage & handling for first book, only $.50 postage
& handling for each additional book.

Enclosed is my check or money order in the amount of $_____

Name_____

Address_____

City_____State_____Zip_____

Please send names and addresses of bookstores and gift shops in your area who might be interested in carrying these books.

_____

_____

_____

_____

_____

_____

_____

_____

_____

_____

Please send names and addresses of bookstores and gift shops in your area who might be interested in carrying these books.

_____

_____

_____

_____

_____

_____

_____

_____

_____

_____

HOLIDAY FAVORITES AND
TASTE OF THE HOLIDAYS
P.O. Box 935
Waycross, Georgia 31502
(912) 285-2848

Please send me_____copies of **HOLIDAY FAVORITES,** $6.95 per copy. Georgia residents add $.42 sales tax.

Please send me_____copies of **TASTE of the HOLIDAYS,** $3.95 per copy. Georgia residents add $.24 sales tax.

Add $1.25 postage & handling for first book, only $.50 postage & handling for each additional book.

Enclosed is my check or money order in the amount of $_____

Name_____

Address_____

City_____State_____Zip_____

- -

HOLIDAY FAVORITES AND
TASTE OF THE HOLIDAYS
P.O. Box 935
Waycross, Georgia 31502
(912) 285-2848

Please send me_____copies of **HOLIDAY FAVORITES,** $6.95 per copy. Georgia residents add $.42 sales tax.

Please send me_____copies of **TASTE of the HOLIDAYS,** $3.95 per copy. Georgia residents add $.24 sales tax.

Add $1.25 postage & handling for first book, only $.50 postage & handling for each additional book.

Enclosed is my check or money order in the amount of $_____

Name_____

Address_____

City_____State_____Zip_____

Please send names and addresses of bookstores and gift shops in your area who might be interested in carrying these books.

_____

_____

_____

_____

_____

_____

_____

_____

Please send names and addresses of bookstores and gift shops in your area who might be interested in carrying these books.

_____

_____

_____

_____

_____

_____

_____

_____